Did you know . . .

. . . that the slave trade brought over
twelve million enslaved Africans across
the Atlantic to the "New World"?

. . . that between 1675 and 1700,
officially recognized slaves in the
North American British colonies jumped
from five thousand to twenty-seven thousand?

. . . that anticolonial and slave uprisings led
to Haiti's establishment in the 1790s as
the second independent nation
in the Western Hemisphere?

. . . nearly two hundred thousand African American
men fought on the side of the Uniòn
during the Civil War?

. . . the first successful desegregation sit-in
happened in a Chicago restaurant in 1943?

. . . the U.S. Census declared in 2003 that
the Latino population in America had,
for the first time, surpassed that
of African Americans?

America I AM
BLACK FACTS

Also by Quintard Taylor

AFRICAN AMERICAN WOMEN CONFRONT THE WEST,
1600–2000

BUFFALO SOLDIER REGIMENT:
HISTORY OF THE TWENTY-FIFTH
UNITED STATES INFANTRY, 1869–1926
(WITH JOHN NANKIVELL)

IN SEARCH OF THE RACIAL FRONTIER:
AFRICAN AMERICANS IN THE WEST, 1528–1990

THE FORGING OF A BLACK COMMUNITY:
SEATTLE'S CENTRAL DISTRICT,
FROM 1870 THROUGH THE CIVIL RIGHTS ERA

Please visit: Hay House USA: **www.hayhouse.com**®
Hay House Australia: **www.hayhouse.com.au**
Hay House UK: **www.hayhouse.co.uk**
Hay House South Africa: **www.hayhouse.co.za**
Hay House India: **www.hayhouse.co.in**

America I AM
BLACK FACTS

THE TIMELINES OF
AFRICAN AMERICAN HISTORY, 1601–2008

QUINTARD TAYLOR

SMILEYBOOKS

Distributed by Hay House, Inc.

CARLSBAD, CALIFORNIA · NEW YORK CITY
LONDON · SYDNEY · JOHANNESBURG
VANCOUVER · HONG KONG · NEW DELHI

Published in the United States by: SmileyBooks, 33 West 19th Street, 4th Floor, New York, NY 10011

Distributed in the United States by: Hay House, Inc.: www.hayhouse.com • **Published and distributed in Australia by:** Hay House Australia Pty. Ltd.: www.hayhouse.com.au • **Published and distributed in the United Kingdom by:** Hay House UK, Ltd.: www.hayhouse.co.uk • **Published and distributed in the Republic of South Africa by:** Hay House SA (Pty), Ltd.: www.hayhouse.co.za • **Distributed in Canada by:** Raincoast: www.raincoast.com • **Published and Distributed in India by:** Hay House Publishers India: www.hayhouse.com

Design: Charles McStravick

Library of Congress Cataloging-in-Publication Data

Taylor, Quintard.
America I am black facts : the timelines of African American history, 1601-2008 / Quintard Taylor.
    p. cm.
Includes bibliographical references.
ISBN 978-1-4019-2406-5 (trade pbk.)
1. African Americans--History--Chronology. I. Title.
E185.T288 2009
973'.0496073--dc22
                                2008046872

ISBN: 978-1-4019-2406-5

12 11 10 09   4 3 2 1
1st edition, February 2009

Printed in the United States of America

TO MY PARENTS,

GRACE AND QUINTARD TAYLOR,

THE FIRST HISTORIANS

I EVER KNEW

CONTENTS

INTRODUCTION

WHY TIMELINES?

Time is the great equalizer. No person, race, culture, or nation stands beyond its reach or can alter its inevitable progress. Timelines, the list of events in chronological order, that is, as they happened, allow us to understand the historical past as that equalizer, in its most basic, elemental form, as the evolution of events, episodes, and eras.

For those who study African American history, which has often been subject to blatant and subtle distortion, mischaracterization, and misunderstanding, a timeline can be both corrective and surprisingly informative. It can show what happened, if not why. *America I AM Black Facts* serves as a starting point for understanding that historical experience. It is, in brief summary, the pivotal moments in the story of the forty million people of African descent in the

United States over the past five centuries. It is also a starting point in the exploration of their relationship with more than one billion black folks around the world. Finally, like the four-year multi-city traveling exhibit, *America I AM: The African American Imprint* inspired by Tavis Smiley, this volume is a synopsis, a book of facts that chronicles the indelible imprint African Americans have made on the life, history, and culture of the United States and the world.

The six timelines presented as separate chapters in this volume provide a perspective that often does not appear in narrative or analytic histories of black America. The year 1892 provides a cogent example. The academic historian usually focuses on 1892 as the year when a record number of people, 161 African Americans and 69 whites, were lynched in the United States. Yet the timeline shows that in the same year, Sissieretta Jones became the first African American to perform at Carnegie Hall, and the National Medical Association was formed in Atlanta. Eighteen hundred ninety-two was also the year that three companies of the Twenty-fifth Infantry, the famous Buffalo Soldiers, were sent by President Benjamin Harrison into northern Idaho to reestablish order following an outbreak of violence by striking white miners and the year that the first intercollegiate football game between black American colleges took place in Charlotte, North Carolina, between Biddle University (now Johnson C. Smith University) and Livingston College. Biddle won the contest, 4–0, on a snow-covered field in Charlotte on December 27. Thus to African Americans living at that time, the seminal event of the year depended upon a host of factors, including one's gender, class status, education, political persuasion, and state or regional home. In other words, the timelines allow us the opportunity to see the world not from our contemporary vantage point looking backward at what we now assume was most important, but more accurately as it might have appeared to those at the time.

Of course for millions of black folks in 1892, the daily struggle to survive overshadowed any and all of these events. Complicating matters further, communication systems in 1892 may have left thousands more unaware of most of these developments. Nonetheless, each event in its own way mattered. Their consequences may or may not have escaped contemporaries, but certainly those consequences would impact the generations that followed.

The communication revolution of the twentieth century quickly ended that isolation even as it presented new challenges to African America. The seven-decade-long great migration of African Americans from the South to the North, or more accurately from the rural South to the urban North, West, and South, ushered in a new period of spatial concentration that facilitated various types of communication. Beginning with the 1920s and 1930s, African Americans created what historians have described as self-conscious black publics. These new publics emerged as more and more African Americans had access to vital information about themselves as well as the United States, Africa, and the rest of the world. Thus they became more willing to openly challenge general media images of themselves, their history, and their culture and to craft counternarratives that reflected their own sense of identity and peoplehood. Coupled with rising levels of education and prosperity, which both caused and were a consequence of civil rights struggles, as well as technological innovations, including mass-circulation newspapers, radio, television, and, most recently, the Internet, more and more African Americans began to shape the collective culture and history of black America and the world beyond. The dramatic increase in the number of twentieth-century entries in chapter 5 reflects this change.

As the twenty-first century unfolds, African America continues to evolve in surprising ways. None is more surprising than the rise of the black immigrant population and especially the African-born population. In many areas of the United States, those who were born on the African continent and migrated here, and their descendants, comprise a growing and significant segment of the population of African descent. Two events recorded in chapters 5 and 6 reflect this profound change. The U.S. Census of 2000 showed 746,000 sub-Saharan Africans living in the United States and about 1.7 million people who were direct descendants of those immigrants. When added to the 3 million people of West Indian ancestry residing in the United States, they comprised 14 percent of the black population. The second event is reflective of the first: the nomination by the Democratic Party of one of those new African Americans, Barack Obama, and his election as the 44th president of the United States.

The history of a distinct group is never created in isolation. *America I AM Black Facts* places the African American past in relation to surrounding and apparently unrelated events. Why else would the founding of Paris be included in such a publication? This chronology of the black American experience begins not with the Declaration of Independence in 1776 or the arrival of the first Africans in St. Augustine in 1565 or in Jamestown in 1619. Instead it commences much earlier, in East Africa, with the beginning of human history. Contemporary DNA research reveals that all human history begins with *Homo sapiens* who first appeared in East Africa around one hundred thousand years ago and shortly afterward began the first global African diaspora from that area. Their migration across and ultimately out of Africa reminds us that regardless of the continent from which our more recent ancestors departed, we are all African in our human ancestry.

The events in Africa, from the emergence of Egypt as a civilized society up to Columbus's landing in what would be called the Americas in 1492, provided the social, political, and cultural environment that helped shape the worldview of the millions of Africans who were forcibly brought to the New World. That worldview in turn, although influenced by other social, political, and cultural forces from Europe as well as those indigenous to the Americas, would in turn shape the perspective of the forty million people of African descent currently residing in the United States. The events of the past, particularly in Africa, thus serve not only as a preface but as a crucible to understanding contemporary African America.

In this present global moment we need to recall not only discrete African American history but its relationship to the rest of the world community. Global events and African American history are inextricably intertwined. The Haitian Revolution at the end of the eighteenth century had a decided impact on U.S. politics, especially on the slavery debate and the Louisiana Purchase. As we see in chapter 3, millions of Americans of all backgrounds currently living in that wide swath of land stretching from the Mississippi River to the headwaters of the Missouri River are there at least in part because of the actions of a few thousand slaves in revolt against their French overlords on the western third of the island of Hispaniola.

The role of African American activists, such as Reverend Leon Sullivan and Randall Robinson, who led millions around the world in challenging apartheid in South Africa, eventually led to the birth of a democratic government elected by all of its people for the first time in that nation's history. Timeline entries in chapter 5 remind us of that complex relationship.

A few cautionary notes are in order. *America I AM Black Facts* provides a skeleton of African American history. It can recount what happened but it does not attempt to explain why. Those who are interested in the process of history, the process by which black women and men challenged their circumstances and the way their ideas and values moved a community or a nation, will have to look elsewhere. We suggest a few places to initiate that search in the bibliography at the end of this book.

Since the 1960s there has been an explosion in the number of books on African American history. Major universities and public libraries have thousands of volumes. My home institution, the University of Washington, for example, had 302 books on black history in 1970. Today it has nearly 5,000 volumes, with approximately five new arrivals each week. For graduate students studying U.S. history, African American history is clearly one of the most important and popular fields.

The Internet also provides voluminous information, although it is of varying quality. BlackPast.org (www.blackpast.org), at more than three thousand pages, is the largest free and ungated Web site devoted to providing the public with reference information on African American history. The Web site provides access to the more than one hundred museums that focus on African American history in thirty states across the nation. It also serves as a gateway to a wealth of information on the black past and supplements the presentation of the America I AM: The African American Imprint traveling museum exhibit.

Every attempt has been made to ensure the accuracy of the information presented in this volume. We have consulted a number of sources and, whenever possible, attempted to resolve disputed material. No timeline, however, is error free. While the dates of events in the post-1500 period can be listed with certainty, events that transpired before that period, especially in Africa and other areas, are often approximations.

Moreover, while every effort has been made to provide a balanced and comprehensive rendering of the hundreds of events that shaped the course of African American history, the selection of those events is itself an arbitrary exercise, influenced by the views and beliefs of the chronicler. Nor can *every* event be listed. We welcome comments (and criticism) from those who feel crucial events have been excluded.

Finally, the importance of a past event is often shaped by the way we view that event in the contemporary era. Many of the key developments that were often said to frame the civil rights era of the 1950s and 1960s seem less important to those who came of age in the 1990s, just as events during World War II resonate less with the contemporaries of the 1960s and 1970s. Timelines cannot cater to fad and fashion in the way historical events are emphasized, but anyone looking at a chronology of events compiled in 1940, 1960, or 1980 quickly recognizes the radically different areas of emphasis. In their brevity and succinctness, timelines can make history alive, accessible, and approachable.

America I AM Black Facts seeks to ensure just that. We believe what is listed in this volume is of enduring significance regardless of differing generational perspectives. In fact, our chronology's most useful contribution to the knowledge base of African American history is its identification of those events of overarching significance. This timeline is then, in its most basic form, an introduction to the rich, complex, tragic, and triumphal history of African Americans over five centuries in what is now the United States. As you read the pages of *America I AM Black Facts,* you will begin that introduction.

Near view of the Great Pyramid of Cheops, Gizeh, Egypt.

CHAPTER ONE

THE AFRICAN FOUNDATION

Timeline: Before 1601

African American history begins much earlier than the
arrival of the first Spanish-speaking black settlers in
what is now the American Southwest in the late 1500s or the
first arrivals in the British colonies in 1619. Those arrivals,
whether slave or free, came from Africa or were descendants
from Africans who resided in Spain or Portugal. These first
black settlers came with values, ideas, beliefs, and worldviews—what would be known collectively as culture—that
originated on the African continent. To be sure, they were
influenced by the Europeans and indigenous cultures they
encountered in the New World, but their cultural foundation was established in Africa.

The question is: Which Africa? The four centuries
of the transatlantic slave trade brought to the New World

over twelve million people from Senegambia (what is now Senegal) south to present-day Angola, but also including peoples from what is now Mozambique and Madagascar. These people came from literally hundreds of small states and some powerful empires. They had little in common in terms of language and culture and, in fact, often forged new collective identities once they arrived in Brazil, Cuba, Jamaica, South Carolina, Rhode Island, or Nova Scotia.

Yet most of these people were influenced either directly or indirectly by widely held religious beliefs, such as Islam, and thus arrived with worldviews intact. This chronology begins with ancient Egypt, the first example of the evolution of these worldviews, and includes references to the emergence of other centralized states and empires, including Ghana, Mali, Songhai, Benin, the Kongo, and Great Zimbabwe and its successor state, Monomotapa. All of these states and their weaker neighbors were peopled by the women and men who would eventually be removed to the Americas.

The chronology, however, is mostly about the New World and illustrates the introduction of the first African peoples into North and South America. Although many of the first arrivals were free, it was clear—with the decision by Spanish king Ferdinand II in 1501 to allow enslaved Africans to be brought to Spain's American colonies—that the growth of European overseas colonial empires and the growth of African enslavement would be inextricably intertwined.

TIMELINE
Before 1601

ca. 4.2 million years ago *Australopithecus anamensis,* the first known hominid ancestor of modern humans, emerges on the shores of what is now Lake Rudolf in East Africa.

ca. 3.2 million years ago The 1974 discovery of the nearly complete hominid skeleton of "Lucy" (*Australopithecus afarensis*), near what is now Hadar, Ethiopia, establishes the origin of human history in this region of East Africa. In 2006, a 3.3-million-year-old fossilized hominid toddler was uncovered in the same region, now known to scientists as the Cradle of Humanity.

ca. 1.8 million years ago *Homo erectus* emerges in East Africa.

ca. 1.7 million years ago Beginning of the migration of hominids (ancestors of modern humans) out of Africa.

ca. 1 million years ago Earliest evidence of the use of fire.

ca. 900,000 years ago Earliest evidence of hominids in Asia.

ca. 850,000 years ago Hominids reach Europe.

ca. 100,000 years ago *Homo sapiens* (anatomically modern humans) emerge in East Africa and soon after begin migrating to Asia and Europe. DNA mapping now indicates that the entire world's population evolved from this first group of humans.

ca. 6500 BCE Cattle domesticated in North Africa and the Sahara region.

ca. 6000 BCE Agriculture emerges along the Nile River.

ca. 4100 BCE Sorghum and rice cultivated in Sudan.

ca. 4000 BCE Egypt emerges as a flourishing civilization.

ca. 3500 BCE Beginning of the Sahara Desert. Saharan agricultural communities migrate north or south in front of the expanding desert.

ca. 3100 BCE First fortified towns are built in Egypt; beginning of urbanization.

ca. 3000 BCE All of Egypt is united under one ruler, King Menes. The capital is established at Memphis.

ca. 2613 BCE First pyramid is built in Egypt.

ca. 2500 BCE Other civilizations emerge in Mesopotamia, northern China, and northeastern India.

Nubia emerges with its capital at Kerma. It soon becomes a rival to Egypt.

The Egyptian calendar divides the day into twenty-four units.

ca. 2000 BCE Egypt conquers Nubia.

ca. 1760 BCE Hammurabi's Code recorded in Mesopotamia, the best-known early written body of law in the world.

ca. 1500 BCE Horses are introduced into Egypt from Southwest Asia.

ca. 1200 BCE Olmec civilization emerges in Mexico. The most famous Olmec ruins are six heads, each measuring eight to nine feet in height, weighing twenty to forty tons and displaying distinctly Negroid features.

ca. 1000 BCE Horses are introduced into sub-Saharan Africa from Egypt.

ca. 920 BCE Nubians establish the state of Kush (in present-day Sudan), with its capital at Napata.

727 BCE King Piankhi of Kush conquers all of Egypt. Kushites rule Egypt until 664 BCE.

671 BCE Assyria conquers Egypt. Kushite rulers retreat to Napata.

ca. 600 BCE Beginnings of Nok culture in the Niger River Valley.

ca. 580 BCE First African production of iron takes place in Meroe, the capital of Kush.

563 BCE Birth of Buddha.

ca. 525 BCE Egypt becomes part of the Persian Empire.

ca. 500 BCE Axum emerges in northeastern Africa.

Peoples from southwest Arabia settle in present-day Ethiopia.

Iron-working techniques reach West Africa.

ca. 400 BCE Iron-working Bantu farmers in what is present-day Nigeria begin a multicentury migration that will spread their language and culture throughout what is now sub-Saharan Africa.

Sphynx and pyramids of Cheffren and Menkaura.

332 BCE Egypt is conquered by Alexander the Great.

256 BCE Romans invade North Africa.

221 BCE Beginning of construction of the Great Wall of China.

200 BCE West African city of Jenne begins as a small settlement on an island in the Niger River.

100 BCE Camels are introduced into the Sahara Desert from Egypt by the Romans.

30 BCE Cleopatra, ruler of Egypt, commits suicide. Egypt is annexed by the Roman Empire.

25 BCE Kushites invade Roman-controlled Egypt. A Roman reprisal raid sacks Napata.

33 Death of Christ, beginnings of the Christian faith.

50 London is founded by the Romans.

60 Roman emperor Nero sends expedition to Meroe, Kush; (present-day Sudan).

ca. 200 Bantu peoples reach the east coast of Africa.

ca. 250 Ghana emerges in West Africa.

ca. 300 Axumites become the first Africans to mint coins.

310 Greek mathematician Diophantus, a resident of Alexandria, Egypt, publishes *Arithmetika*, which introduces the concept of algebra.

333 King Ezana of Axum (early Ethiopia) converts to Christianity.

350 King Ezana conquers Meroe (Kush).

375 Attila the Hun invades Europe.

385 Copper mining and smelting begin at Kansanshi on the present-day Congo–Zambia border.

ca. 400 Seafaring peoples from Indonesia begin settling on the island of Madagascar.

ca. 450 Axum reaches the height of its power in northeastern Africa.

476 End of the Roman Empire.

ca. 500 Bantu farmers reach present-day South Africa.

Beginning of the salt and gold camel caravan trade between Ghana and North Africa.

ca. 525 Axumites conquer Yemen, defeating its Jewish rulers and reestablishing Christianity as the dominant faith in the region.

540 Ethiopian monks begin to translate the Bible into their language.

550 Farming communities emerge in South Africa.

570 Kingdom of Kanem–Bornu is established on Lake Chad in West Africa.

622 Mohammad marches from Mecca to Medina, initiating the Muslim faith.

634 Arab Muslims begin the first attempt to conquer Axum.

ca. 650 Arab traders establish the first Islamic cities on the east coast of Africa.

652 Christian Nubians and Arab Muslims agree that Aswan on the Nile River will be the southern boundary of Muslim rule.

702 Axumites invade Arabia, attack the city of Jeddah, and eventually extend their control over much of the southern Arabian peninsula.

711 Arabs conquer and control all of North Africa and most of the Iberian Peninsula (present-day Spain and Portugal).

732 Muslim forces are defeated by Frankish and Burgundian forces at the Battle of Tours in central France. They retreat to the Iberian Peninsula, which they occupy for seven hundred years.

745 Christian Nubians and Ethiopians invade and temporarily occupy Cairo, the capital of Muslim Egypt.

ca. 750 Islam is introduced in West Africa.

753 Arabian expedition reaches Ghana in West Africa.

ca. 825 East African market towns in present-day Kenya, Tanzania, and Zanzibar engage in trade with Arabs and Persians.

ca. 850 Gunpowder is invented in China.

Citadel of Great Zimbabwe is built in southern Africa.

951 Paris is founded.

960 Falasha (Ethiopian Jewish) warriors conquer the city of Axum.

975 Christian Axum is conquered by Muslims.

998 Kano, the first of the Hausa city-states, emerges in what is now northern Nigeria.

1054 Berber leader Abu Bakr establishes the Almoravid Empire; founds the city of Marrakech in 1070.

1056 Almoravids conquer southern Spain.

1076 Almoravids conquer Kumbi–Saleh, the capital of the Empire of Ghana.

1096 The first Crusade to the Holy Land.

1117 City of Lalibela becomes the capital of Christian Ethiopia. Beginning of the construction of rock-cut churches.

1139 Igbo culture emerges in what is now southeastern Nigeria.

1150 The Zagwe Dynasty emerges in Ethiopia. The new rulers are determined to build a larger, more powerful state than Axum.

ca. 1175 Ife culture emerges around the city of Ile–Ife, established as a village around 500 in present-day southwest Nigeria.

ca. 1200 Monomotapa emerges as a centralized state in present-day Zimbabwe.

1209 University of Cambridge is founded in England.

1235 The Empire of Mali emerges in West Africa under Sundiata.

1255 Kingdom of Benin established on the west coast of Africa in present-day Nigeria.

1260 By this date, the city of Timbuktu is the religious, commercial, and political center of the Empire of Mali.

1271–95 Marco Polo travels to China.

1324–25 Pilgrimage of Mansa Musa, ruler of the Mali Empire, to Mecca. This is the apogee of the Mali Empire.

1325 Aztecs establish the city of Tenochtitlán as the capital of their empire in Mexico.

1340 Building of the Great Mosque at Jenne in the Mali Empire.

1364 Norman navigators reach the mouth of the Senegal River. They are the first known Europeans to reach sub-Saharan Africa.

1375 The Kingdom of Songhai breaks away from Mali Empire.

1390 The Kingdom of Kongo (in present-day Congo and Angola) emerges in central Africa.

1400 By this date a flourishing slave trade exists in the Mediterranean World. Most of the slaving countries are Italian principalities, such as Florence and Venice. Most of those enslaved are Greeks and Eastern Europeans. Between 1414 and 1423, ten thousand Eastern European slaves are sold in Venice alone.

1410 Hausa cavalry is the first in Africa equipped with iron weaponry and armor.

1415 An ambassador from the East African trading city of Malindi reaches China.

1421 Ships from Ming China establish trading contact with cities of East Africa.

1427 Ethiopian emperor Yeshaq sends envoys to Aragon in Spain to forge an alliance of Christian states against Islam.

1431 Ming admiral Zheng reaches Malindi and establishes a trade in silk, gold, and animal skins.

1434 The Portuguese establish trading outposts along the West African coast.

1441 Antam Goncalvez of Portugal captures Africans in what is now Senegal, initiating direct European involvement in the African slave trade.

Act of Union signed between the Church of Ethiopia and the Church of Rome.

1444 Lancarote de Freitas, a tax collector from the Portuguese town of Lagos, forms a company to trade in African slaves. His company captures 235 Africans, who are brought to Lagos and sold. This is the first large group of slaves brought to the Iberian Peninsula by Portuguese Christians.

1450 Sankore University founded at Timbuktu.

1452 Sugar plantations established by the Portuguese on the Madeira Islands use African slaves exclusively for the first time.

1453 The Ottoman Turks capture Constantinople and thus divert the trade in Eastern European slaves away from the Mediterranean to Islamic markets. The Italians increasingly look to North Africa as their source for slaves.

1462 Portuguese traders bring slaves to Seville in Spain for the first time.

1468 Mali conquered by the Empire of Songhai.

1470 By this point small vineyards and sugar plantations have emerged around Naples and on the island of Sicily, with Africans as the primary enslaved people providing the labor on these estates.

1471 Portuguese establish a trading post at El Mina on the coast of Ghana.

1481 Portuguese build the Fort of São Jorge to defend El Mina from other European powers.

1483 Portugal and the Kingdom of the Kongo begin a trading partnership. Two years later five Portuguese missionaries arrive in the Kongo.

1486 Portuguese settle the uninhabited West African island of São Tomé. They establish sugar plantations worked exclusively by African slaves brought from the mainland. São Tomé becomes the model for Portuguese plantations in Brazil.

1490 Small populations of free and enslaved Africans extend across the Mediterranean from Sicily to Portugal.

King Nkuwu of the Kongo converts to Christianity.

1492 Spain, under the dual monarchs Ferdinand II and Isabella, capture Grenada and defeat the last Muslim forces on the Iberian Peninsula. Following that victory, the Spanish monarchs require all Jews and Muslims to convert to Christianity or be exiled.

Christopher Columbus makes his first voyage to the New World, opening a vast new empire for plantation slavery.

1493 Muhammad Askia becomes the ruler of the Songhai Empire and establishes the new capital at Gao on the Niger River.

1494 The first Africans arrive in Hispaniola with Christopher Columbus. They are free persons.

1496 Columbus returns to Spain with thirty Native American slaves.

1499 Amerigo Vespucci (whose name is the source for the term "America") takes two hundred Native American slaves from the northern coast of South America to sell in the Spanish port of Cadiz.

1501 Spanish king Ferdinand II allows the intro-duction of enslaved Africans into Spain's American colonies.

1502 The first slaves are taken from Africa to Spanish colonies in the New World.

1504 Christian Nubia is conquered by Islamic forces.

A small group of Africans, probably slaves, are brought to the court of King James IV of Scotland.

1505 Sugarcane is introduced by the Spanish into Santo Domingo (the Dominican Republic).

1509 Ethiopia and Portugal exchange ambassadors.

1513 Thirty Africans accompany Vasco Núez de Balboa on his trip to the Pacific Ocean.

1517 Bishop Bartolomé de Las Casas petitions Spain to allow the importation of twelve enslaved Africans for each household immigrating to America's Spanish colonies. De Las Casas later regrets his actions and becomes an opponent of slavery.

King Charles V of Spain grants the first licenses to import enslaved Africans to the Americas.

1518 King Charles V grants Flemish merchant Lorenzo de Gorrevod permission to import up to four thousand African slaves into New

Spain. Soon afterward the first shipload of enslaved Africans directly from Africa arrives in the West Indies. Prior to this time, Africans were brought first to Europe. From this point thousands of African slaves are sent to the New World each year.

1519 Hernán Cortés begins his conquest of the Aztec Empire. Black Spaniards are among the conquistadors.

1520 Enslaved Africans are now used as laborers in Puerto Rico, Cuba, and Mexico.

1522 African slaves stage a rebellion in Hispaniola. This is the first slave uprising in the New World.

1524 Nearly three hundred African slaves are taken to Cuba to work in local gold mines.

1526 Spanish colonists led by Lucas Vásquez de Ayllón build the community of San Miguel de Guadalupe in what is now Georgia. They bring along enslaved Africans, considered to be the first in the present-day United States. These

Africans flee the colony, however, and make their homes with local Indians. After Ayllón's death, the remaining Spaniards relocate to Hispaniola.

1527–1539 Esteban, a Moroccan-born Muslim slave, explores what is now the southwestern United States.

1529 Alessandro di Medici, the son of an African mother and Lorenzo di Medici, the ruler of the Italian city-state of Urbino, is named the first Duke of Florence by Pope Clement VII.

1532 William Hawkins becomes the first English mariner to visit the coast of West Africa, although he does not take part in slave trading.

1540 An African from Hernando de Soto's expedition decides to remain behind to make his home among the Native Americans there.

Africans serve in the New Mexico expeditions of Francisco Vásquez de Coronado and Hernando de Alarcón.

1542 The Spanish Crown abolishes Indian slavery in its colonial possessions.

1550 The first slaves directly from Africa arrive in the Brazilian city of Salvador.

1562 An expedition to Hispaniola led by John Hawkins, the first English slave trader, sparks English interest in that activity. Hawkins's travels also call attention to Sierra Leone. Hawkins is knighted in 1588 for his service in England's victory over the Spanish Armada.

1565 African farmers and artisans accompany Pedro Menéndez de Avilés on the expedition that establishes the community of San Agustín (St. Augustine, Florida).

1570 New Spain's (Colonial Mexico) population includes 20,569 blacks and 2,439 mulattoes (people of combined African, European, and Native American ancestry).

1573 Professor Bartolomé de Albornoz of the University of Mexico writes against the enslavement and sale of Africans.

1591 Fall of the Empire of Songhai.

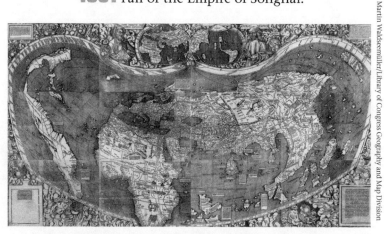

"Universalis Cosmographia Secundum Ptholomaei Traditionem et Americi Vespucii Alioru[m]que Lustrationes," St. Dié, 1507.

1592 The Dutch enter the slave trade.

1594 The French enter the slave trade.

1598 Isabel de Olvera, a free mulatto, accompanies the Juan Guerra de Resa Expedition, which colonizes what is now New Mexico.

Italian map of Africa circa A.D. 1600.

CHAPTER TWO

CREATING NEW WORLD COMMUNITIES

Timeline: 1601–1700

The enslavement of Africans in what would become the United States effectively began in the seventeenth century. Although the Spanish brought enslaved Africans and free blacks to their colonies in the Caribbean and Mexico in the sixteenth century, slavery became rooted in the British North American colonies (what would become the early United States) in the period after the arrival of the first Africans in Jamestown in 1619, the year before the Pilgrims first reached Massachusetts.

Although historians usually characterize the enslavement of Africans as beginning with that landing of twenty blacks, brought to Jamestown by a Dutch vessel, in fact slavery in British North America developed in a halting, haphazard fashion and was not formally fixed until the 1660s. Nor did it involve the tens of thousands or millions of later centuries. By 1675, the time of Bacon's Rebellion, there were only about five thousand enslaved Africans in British North America. Twenty-five years later, in 1700, an informal census of the British North American colonies showed only twenty-seven thousand enslaved persons, which included a number of Native Americans as well as Africans.

Despite the small numbers, human bondage was clearly being instituted on British American (and Dutch American) soil throughout the century. In 1626, for example, the first enslaved Africans arrived in New Amsterdam (now New York City). Three years later the first enslaved Africans arrived in Connecticut. In 1634 slavery was introduced in Maryland and in 1641 Massachusetts legalized the enslavement of blacks, Indians, and, ironically, whites.

The year 1664 proved crucial in the march toward enslavement. By that point, Virginia, the richest and most populous British North American colony, enacted a series of laws that enslaved Africans for life. Maryland, New York, and New Jersey followed with their own variations of lifetime enslavement legislation. By 1690 all British colonies in North America had enslaved Africans. It is also worth noting that in 1688, Quakers in Germantown, Pennsylvania, recorded the first formal protest against slavery in British North America.

The march toward slavery, however, is not the whole story. Throughout the century there were indications of alternative possibilities, of paths not taken regarding enslavement, including some surprising events often ignored by the grand historical narrative of slavery.

In 1624, William Tucker, the first free-born black child in the British colonies, was baptized. Tucker was part of a free black population that originated with the landing of the first twenty blacks in Jamestown, indicating that most of the earliest black arrivals in Virginia were never enslaved. In 1641, Mathias De Sousa, a former African indentured servant, was elected to the Maryland General Assembly, thus becoming the first person of African ancestry to hold office in what would become the United States.

Anthony Johnson, however, was the singular example of the ambiguity of the early racial order in the British colonies. Born free in Africa, Johnson arrived in Virginia in 1621 and for the next twenty years worked as an indentured servant. By 1651 he and his wife, Mary, now freed of indenture, owned 250 acres of land. Showing little concern for the status of fellow Africans, Johnson had acquired two slaves to work his tobacco fields. Yet Johnson's oldest son, Richard, was not allowed by local authorities to inherit the family land upon his father's death in 1669 because Johnson "was a Negroe and by consequence an alien." Johnson's descendants were never enslaved but they remained landless tenant farmers; they never replicated the prosperity of Anthony and Mary Johnson. Their saga was a telltale indication of what would be in store for Africans who somehow escaped formal enslavement.

TIMELINE
1601–1700

1602 By Spanish law, mulattoes, convicts, and "idle" Africans may be shipped to Latin America and forced to work in the mines there.

1607 Jamestown is founded in Virginia.

1609 Fugitive slaves in Mexico, led by Yanga, sign a truce with Spanish colonial authorities and obtain their freedom and a town of their own.

1617 The town of San Lorenzo de los Negros receives a charter from Spanish colonial officials in Mexico and becomes the first officially recognized free settlement for blacks in the New World.

1619 Approximately twenty blacks from a Dutch slaver are purchased as indentured workers for the English settlement of Jamestown. These are the first Africans in the English North American colonies.

Illustration from *Harper's Monthly Magazine,* January 1901, depicting slaves brought to the Jamestown Colony in Virginia in 1619.

1620 The Pilgrims reach New England.

1624 The first African American child born free in the English colonies, William Tucker, is baptized in Virginia.

1626 The first enslaved Africans arrive in the Dutch Colony of New Amsterdam (now New York City).

1629 The first enslaved Africans arrive in what is now Connecticut.

1634 Slavery is introduced in Maryland.

1638 France's North American colonies are opened to trade in enslaved Africans.

1641 Massachusetts explicitly permits slavery of Indians, whites, and Negroes in its "Body of Liberties."

1641 Mathias de Sousa, an African indentured servant who came from England with Lord Baltimore, is elected to Maryland's General Assembly.

1642 Virginia passes a fugitive slave law. Offenders helping runaway slaves are fined in pounds of tobacco. An enslaved person is to be branded with a large "R" after a second escape attempt.

When a French privateer brings to New Netherlands some Africans taken from a Spanish ship, they are sold as slaves because of their race, despite their claims to be free.

1643 The New England Confederation reaches an agreement that makes the signature of a magistrate sufficient evidence to reenslave a suspected fugitive slave.

1645 Merchant ships from Barbados arrive in Boston where they trade their cargoes of enslaved Africans for sugar and tobacco. The profitability of this exchange encourages the slave trade in New England.

ca. 1645 Dutch colonists transfer some of their landholdings in New Amsterdam to their former enslaved Africans as compensation for their support in battles with Native Americans. A condition of the land transfer, however, is the guarantee of a specified amount of food from those lands to their former owners.

1646 New Spain's (Colonial Mexico) population includes 35,089 blacks and 116,529 mulattoes.

1650 Connecticut legalizes slavery. Rhode Island by this date has large plantations worked by enslaved Africans.

1651 Anthony Johnson, a free African American, imports several enslaved Africans and is given a grant of land on Virginia's Pungoteague River. Other free African Americans follow this pattern.

1652 Massachusetts enacts a law requiring all African American and Native American servants to undergo military training so as to be able to help defend the colony.

1655 Anthony Johnson successfully sues for the return of his slave John Casor, whom the court had earlier treated as an indentured servant.

1656 Fearing the potential for slave uprisings, Massachusetts reverses its 1652 statute and prohibits blacks from arming or training as militia. New Hampshire and New York soon follow.

1660 A Connecticut law prohibits African Americans from serving in the militia.

1662 Virginia reverses the presumption of English law that the child follows the status of the father, and enacts a law that makes the free or enslaved status of children dependent on the status of the mother.

1663 Black and white indentured servants plan a rebellion in Gloucester County, Virginia. Their plans are discovered and the leaders are executed.

Maryland authorities declare that all Africans arriving in the colony are presumed to be slaves. Free European American women who marry enslaved men lose their freedom. Children of European American women and enslaved men are enslaved. Other North American colonies develop similar laws.

In South Carolina every new white settler is granted twenty acres for each black male slave and ten acres for each black female slave he or she brings into the colony.

1664 In Virginia, the enslaved African's status is clearly differentiated from the indentured servant's status for the first time when colonial laws decree that enslavement is for life and the condition is transferred to the children through the mother. The terms "black" and "slave" become synonymous, and enslaved Africans are subject to harsher and more brutal control than other laborers.

Maryland establishes slavery for life for persons of African ancestry.

New York and New Jersey also recognize the legality of slavery.

1667 England for the first time enacts strict laws regarding enslaved Africans in its North American mainland colonies. An enslaved African is forbidden to leave the plantation without a pass, and never on Sunday. An enslaved African may not possess weapons or signaling mechanisms, such as horns or whistles. Punishment for an owner who kills an enslaved African is a fifteen-pound fine.

Virginia declares that baptism does not free a slave from bondage, thereby abandoning the Christian tradition of not enslaving other Christians.

1670 A law is enacted in Virginia that all non-Christians who arrive by ship are to be enslaved. A French royal decree brings French shippers into the transatlantic slave trade, with the rationale that the labor of enslaved Africans helps the growth of France's island colonies.

The Massachusetts legislature passes a law that enables its citizens to sell the children of enslaved Africans into bondage, thus separating them from their parents.

1671 A Maryland law states that the conversion of enslaved African Americans to Christianity does not affect their status as enslaved people.

1672 King Charles II of England charters the Royal African Company, which dominates the slave trade to British North America for the next half century.

1673 The Massachusetts legislature passes a law that forbids European Americans from engaging in any trade or commerce with African Americans.

1675 An estimated one hundred thousand Africans are enslaved in the West Indies and another five thousand are in British North America.

1676 Nathaniel Bacon leads an unsuccessful rebellion of whites and blacks against the English colonial government in Virginia.

1681 Maryland laws mandate that children of European servant women and enslaved African men are free, reversing a 1663 statute that enslaved them.

1682 A new slave code in Virginia prohibits weapons for slaves, requires passes beyond the limits of the plantation, and forbids self-defense by any African Americans against any European American.

1685 New York law forbids enslaved Africans and Native Americans from having meetings or carrying firearms.

1688 Quakers in Germantown, Pennsylvania, denounce slavery in the first recorded formal protest in North America against the enslavement of Africans.

1690 By this year, all English colonies in America have enslaved Africans.

Enslaved Africans and Native Americans in Massachusetts plan a rebellion.

1692 The Virginia House of Burgesses enacts the Runaway Slave Law, making it legal to kill a runaway in the course of apprehension.

1693 All fugitive Africans who have escaped slavery in the British colonies and fled to Florida are granted their freedom by the Spanish monarchy.

1694 The introduction of rice into the Carolina colony, ironically from West Africa, increases the need for labor for emerging plantations. This adds another factor to the economic justification and rationalization for expanding the slave trade.

1696 American Quakers, at their annual meeting, warn members against holding Africans in slavery. Violators who continue to keep slaves are threatened with expulsion.

1700 A census reports more than twenty-seven thousand enslaved people, mostly Africans, in the English colonies in North America. The vast majority of these bonds-people live in the southern colonies.

Boston slave traders are involved in selling enslaved Africans in the New England colonies and Virginia.

Massachusetts chief justice Samuel Sewall publishes *The Selling of Joseph,* a book that advances both the economic and moral reasons for the abolition of the trade in enslaved Africans.

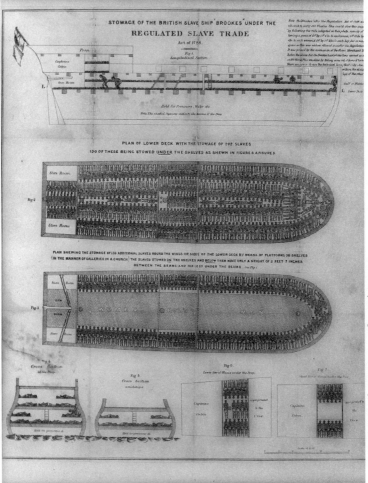

Illustration showing deck plans and cross sections
of British slave ship "Brookes."

CHAPTER THREE

THE WORLD OF THE ENSLAVED

Timeline: 1701–1800

When the eighteenth century began, the United States of America did not exist. There was slavery, however. Thousands of persons of African ancestry—not only in the still evolving British North American colonies but in areas that stretched from present-day Canada to Argentina—knew life only as bondservants.

Given what appeared to be the apparent universality of black enslavement, at least in the New World, and the fact that the numbers of enslaved, whether in Virginia or Brazil, were being steadily augmented by the arrival of thousands of Africans directly from that continent, it would be understandable if black people resigned themselves to the inevitability of their collective fate. Yet they did not. Just as surely as there were black slaves from Nova

Scotia to the Pampas, there was also resistance to slavery in every area where slaves resided. That resistance, often in the form of revolt, left slaveholders unsure of their power and security, and gave hope to those in bondage that freedom, however remote, was nonetheless possible.

That hope inspired rebels in New York City in 1712 and in South Carolina in 1739 to risk their lives for liberty. The grand example of rebellion, however, was the Haitian Revolution. Beginning in 1791, this revolution was both a massive slave uprising and an early anticolonial struggle that would create the second independent nation in the Western Hemisphere. In that regard, the revolution was a melding of the campaigns for individual *and* national freedom.

Most blacks in the New World did not gain their freedom. Their struggle, nonetheless, inspired the few free blacks in these societies to clandestinely help their enslaved brethren while, whenever possible, calling on slaveholders to end their ownership of other human beings. The recognition of the injustice of slavery, and the understanding that their own safety and security were in jeopardy as long as slavery lasted, prompted a small but steadily growing number of whites to challenge the institution as well. The nineteen white citizens of colonial Darien, Georgia, who in 1739 called slavery "shocking to human nature" while requesting a continued ban on slave importations into the colony, reflected an early recognition of the dilemma slavery posed for whites as well as blacks.

That dilemma was reflected in the debates central to the founding of the United States in the 1770s and 1780s. It was the British who were the imperial power determined to keep the American colonies in what they considered political enslavement. Yet the British were responsible for the liberation of thousands of black women and men during and immediately after the American Revolution, whereas patriot leaders vacillated on the question of black freedom and black citizenship. This contradiction was recognized by the enslaved, the British, and on occasion by the patriots themselves.

Thus much of the history of African Americans in the eighteenth century reflects that remarkable and often improbable struggle of the enslaved to be free and of growing numbers of people, black and white, male and female, who gave their energies, resources, and, on occasion, their lives to bring about that freedom.

TIMELINE
1701–1800

1704 French colonist Elias Neau opens a school for enslaved African Americans in New York City.

1708 Africans in the colony of South Carolina outnumber Europeans, making it the first English colony with a black majority.

1711 Great Britain's Queen Anne overrules a Pennsylvania colonial law prohibiting slavery.

1712 The New York City slave revolt begins on April 6. Nine whites are killed and an unknown number of blacks die in the uprising. Colonial authorities execute twenty-one slaves. Six enslaved people commit suicide.

1713 England secures the exclusive right to transport slaves to the Spanish colonies in America.

1718 The French found New Orleans in their colonial possession, Louisiana.

1721 South Carolina limits the vote to free white Christian men.

Onesimus, an enslaved African in Massachusetts Colony, describes to Cotton Mather the African method of inoculation against smallpox. The technique is used to protect patriot soldiers in the American Revolution and is later perfected by British physician Edward Jenner in the 1790s.

1724 Louisiana's *Code Noir* is enacted in New Orleans to regulate black slavery and to banish Jews from the colony.

Boston imposes a curfew on non-whites.

1727 Enslaved Africans and Native Americans revolt in Middlesex and Gloucester counties in the Virginia colony.

1733 Spain promises freedom in Spanish Florida to slaves who escape from the English colonies.

1735 The colony of South Carolina passes laws requiring enslaved people to wear clothing identifying them as slaves. Freed slaves are required to leave the colony within six months or risk reenslavement.

1737 An indentured black servant petitions a Massachusetts court and wins his freedom after the death of his master.

1739 The first major South Carolina slave revolt takes place in Stono on September 9. Twenty whites and more than twice as many black slaves are killed as the armed slaves try to flee to Florida.

Nineteen white citizens of Darien, Georgia, petition the colonial governor to continue the ban on the importation of Africans into the colony, calling African enslavement "shocking to human nature." This is the first antislavery protest in the southern colonies. Ten years later, however, Georgia authorities repeal the ban.

1741 During the New York Slave Conspiracy Trials, New York City officials execute thirty-four people for planning to burn down the town. Thirteen African American men are burned at the stake and another seventeen black men, two white men, and two white women are hanged. Seventy blacks and seven whites are permanently expelled from the city.

South Carolina's colonial legislature enacts a law banning the teaching of enslaved people to read and write.

1742 New Spain's (colonial Mexico) population includes 20,131 blacks and 266,196 mulattoes.

1746 Lucy Terry, a slave, composes "Bars Fight," the first known poem by an African American. A description of an Indian raid on Terry's hometown of Deerfield in colonial Massachusetts, the poem is passed down orally and published in 1855.

1751 Colonial South Carolina prohibits slaves from learning about or practicing medicine.

1752 Twenty-one-year-old Benjamin Banneker of Maryland constructs one of the earliest clocks in colonial America, the first of his many inventions and innovations. He dies in 1806.

Future president George Washington acquires the Mount Vernon plantation and eighteen enslaved people in northern Virginia. Eventually he and his wife own two hundred bondservants.

1758 The African Baptist or "Bluestone" Church is founded on the William Byrd plantation near the Bluestone River, in Mecklenburg, Virginia, becoming the first known black church in North America.

A school for free black children opens in Philadelphia.

1760 Jupiter Hammon of Long Island, New York, publishes a book of poetry. This is believed to be the first volume written and published by an African American.

The black population in the British American colonies is estimated at 325,000.

1770 Crispus Attucks, an escaped slave, becomes the first colonial resident to die for American independence when he is killed by the British in the Boston Massacre.

Portrait of Crispus Attucks, killed during the Boston Massacre in 1770.

W.H. Card/Library of Congress Prints and Photographs Division

1772 On June 22, Lord Chief Mansfield rules in the James Somerset case that an enslaved person brought to England becomes free and cannot be returned to slavery. His ruling establishes the legal basis for the freeing of England's fifteen thousand slaves.

1773 Phillis Wheatley of Boston publishes *Poems on Various Subjects, Religious and Moral.* This is the first book of poetry published by an African American woman.

Illustration from *Poems on Various Subjects, Religious and Moral* by Phillis Wheatley.

Scipio Moorhead/Library of Congress Rare Book and Special Collections Division

The Silver Bluff Baptist Church, the oldest continuously operating black church, is founded in Silver Bluff, South Carolina, near Savannah, Georgia. (The first African Baptist Church of Savannah also claims this distinction.)

1774 A group of blacks petitions the Massachusetts General Court (legislature), insisting that they too have a natural right to their freedom.

1775–81 The American War of Independence. Approximately 450,000 enslaved Africans comprise 20 percent of the population of the colonies at the time of the Declaration of Independence.

1775 African Americans participate on the patriot side in the earliest battles of the Revolution: Concord, Lexington, and Bunker Hill.

General George Washington reverses his earlier policy of rejecting the services of slaves and free blacks in the army. Five thousand African Americans serve during the Revolutionary War in integrated units, such as the Minutemen and Ethan Allen's Green Mountain Boys. Two predominantly black units are organized in Massachusetts, another in Connecticut, and one in Rhode Island.

The first Abolition Society meeting in North America is held Philadelphia; Benjamin Franklin is elected president of the society.

On November 7, Lord Dunmore, British governor of Virginia, declares all slaves free who come to the defense of the British Crown against the patriot forces. Dunmore eventually organizes the first regiment of black soldiers, called Dunmore's Ethiopian Regiment, to fight under the British flag.

1776 A passage authored by Thomas Jefferson condemning the slave trade is removed from the Declaration of Independence due to pressure from the southern colonies.

Approximately one hundred thousand enslaved people flee their masters during the Revolution.

The Society of Friends (Quakers) in England and Pennsylvania require members to free slaves or face expulsion.

1777 Vermont abolishes slavery.

1778 Boston businessman Paul Cuffe and his brother, John, refuse to pay taxes, claiming that as blacks not allowed to vote, they suffer taxation without representation.

1779 Titus Cornelius, more commonly known as Colonel Tye, is one of the most prominent black guerrilla fighters supporting the British during the American Revolution. This former Virginia slave becomes a captain in Lord Dunmore's Ethiopian Regiment in 1778. The following summer he leads black and white loyalists in New Jersey in a series of raids on patriot positions. Colonel Tye dies of battle wounds in 1789.

1780 Massachusetts abolishes slavery and grants African American men the right to vote.

The Free African Union Society is created in Newport, Rhode Island. It is the first cultural organization established by blacks in North America.

Pennsylvania adopts the first gradual emancipation law. All children of enslaved people born after November 1, 1780, will be free on their twenty-eighth birthday.

1781–83 Twenty thousand black loyalists depart with British troops from the newly independent United States. Approximately five thousand African Americans served with patriot forces. Three times that many served with the British, although not all of them leave the new nation.

1781 Los Angeles, California, is founded by fifty-four settlers, including twenty-six of African ancestry.

1783 James Durham, born enslaved in 1762, learns medicine from white doctors who first teach him to read. Durham buys his freedom and begins a medical practice in New Orleans. He is considered the first African American medical doctor.

The *Gregson v. Gilbert* case is decided by Lord Mansfield. While transporting 470 slaves from West Africa to Jamaica on the slave ship *Zong* in 1781, Captain Luke Collingwood threw overboard 132 sick slaves and attempted to collect insurance on them. The insurance underwriter refused and the case was brought before Lord

Chief Mansfield, the highest-ranking jurist in Great Britain, who ruled against the shipowners. The case helped generate sympathy for the evolving abolitionist cause in England and the United States.

1784 Connecticut and Rhode Island adopt gradual emancipation laws.

Congress rejects Thomas Jefferson's proposal to exclude slavery from all western territories after 1800.

1785 New York frees all slaves who served in the Revolutionary Army.

1787 Congress enacts the Northwest Ordinance, which establishes formal procedures for transforming territories into states. It provides for the eventual establishment of three to five states in the area north of the Ohio River, to be considered equal with the original thirteen. The ordinance includes a Bill of Rights that guarantees freedom of religion, the right to trial by jury, public education, and a ban on slavery in the region.

The U.S. Constitution is drafted. It calls for the continuation of the slave trade for another twenty years and requires states to aid slaveholders in the recovery of fugitive slaves. It also stipulates that a slave counts as three-fifths of a man for purposes of determining representation in the House of Representatives.

Free blacks in New York City found the African Free School, where future leaders Henry Highland Garnett and Alexander Crummell are educated.

Richard Allen and Absalom Jones form the Free African Society in Philadelphia.

Prince Hall, who led fifteen other free blacks in forming African Lodge No. 1 of the Masons in 1775, becomes Worshipful Master when the lodge charter arrives from London. African Lodge No. 1 becomes the first recognized Masonic lodge in the United States consisting exclusively of African Americans.

The Society for the Abolition of the Slave Trade is formed in London, England. This is the first abolitionist organization in Europe.

1788 The Massachusetts General Court (legislature), following an incident in which free blacks were kidnapped and transported to the island of Martinique, declares the slave trade illegal and provides monetary damages to victims of kidnappings.

1789 The French Revolution begins.

1790 First census of the United States.
U.S. population: 3,929,214
Black population: 757,208 (19.3 percent), including 59,557 free African Americans.

Free African Americans in Charleston form the Brown Fellowship Society.

1791 The Haitian Revolution begins.

1793 The United States Congress enacts the first Fugitive Slave Law. Providing assistance to fugitive slaves is now a criminal offense.

Eli Whitney patents the cotton gin on March 13, which begins the slave labor-based "cotton economy" of the South.

Philadelphia's First African Methodist Episcopal Church, also known as Mother Bethel AME Church, is founded.

1794 The French government abolishes slavery. The law is repealed by Napoleon in 1802.

New York adopts a gradual emancipation law.

1793 New Spain's population includes 6,100 blacks and 369,790 mulattoes.

1795 Bowdoin College is founded in Maine. It later becomes a center for abolitionist activity; General Oliver O. Howard, for whom Howard University would later be named, graduated from the college; Harriet Beecher Stowe taught there and began to write *Uncle Tom's Cabin* while there in 1850.

1796 On August 23, the African Methodist Episcopal Church is organized in Philadelphia.

1800 Census of 1800.
U.S. population: 5,308,483
Black population: 1,002,037 (18.9 percent), including 108,435 free African Americans.

Gabriel Prosser attempts a slave rebellion in Virginia.

The Congress of the United States bars U.S. citizens from exporting slaves.

The United States Congress rejects 85 to 1 an antislavery petition offered by free Philadelphia African Americans.

Illustration from *The Graphic* June 7, 1884
depicting East Africans rescued from a slave vessel.

CHAPTER FOUR

THE DESTRUCTION OF SLAVERY

Timeline: 1801–1900

Slavery and freedom were the hallmarks of the nine-teenth-century African American experience. At the beginning of the century, 89 percent of the one million blacks in the United States were enslaved, a condition that had overwhelmingly dominated black life in North America since the early 1600s. By the sixth decade of the century, the Civil War engulfed the entire United States and freed four million African American women and men.

Black men and women assisted in their liberation. Nearly two hundred thousand African American men fought for the Union and thousands of black women—such as the Ladies Refugee Aid Society of Lawrence, Kansas—used their collective resources to help ensure that freedom. The state-ment of South Carolina Reconstruction-era black politician

Daniel Corbin in 1871 captured the dramatic transformation over the past decade. He said, "We have lived over a century in the last ten years."

The dream of freedom heretofore imagined only by the enslaved millions and a few thousand abolitionists, including most notably Frederick Douglass, Sojourner Truth, and Harriet Tubman, who supported them, now became a reality. That reality, however, was quickly put to the test by Reconstruction.

For one brief historical moment in the long, tortured odyssey of African America, Reconstruction promised not only political freedom but full citizenship. Black men from Virginia to Texas, and the African American women who supported them and often organized and orchestrated their efforts, sought through the ballot box to make Reconstruction not simply the process of bringing ex-Confederate states back into the Union but a means to ensure that new citizenship was meaningful and practical in their lives. Many of these men, only a few years away from slavery's lash, created constitutions and crafted laws designed to make permanent the promise of freedom.

Ultimately these political and racial reformers were swept from office, but not before providing African America with a vision of what a truly democratic America could be. That vision would inspire millions of others in the twentieth and twenty-first centuries.

TIMELINE
1801–1900

1802 The Ohio Constitution outlaws slavery. It also prohibits free blacks from voting. The Ohio Legislature passes the first "Black Laws," which place other restrictions on free African Americans living in the state.

James Callender claims that Thomas Jefferson has "for many years past kept, as his concubine, one of his own slaves," Sally Hemings. His charge is published in the Richmond *Recorder* that month, and the story is soon picked up by the Federalist press around the country.

1803 On April 30, Louisiana is purchased from the French. The new territory nearly doubles the size of the United States.

1804 On January 1, Haiti becomes an independent nation. It is the second independent nation in the Western Hemisphere (after the United States).

1804–06 The Lewis and Clark Expedition explores newly purchased Louisiana and the Pacific Northwest. An African American, York is prominent in the expedition.

1807 Great Britain abolishes the importation of enslaved Africans into its colonial possessions.

New Jersey disenfranchises black male voters and all women voters.

1808 The United States government abolishes the importation of enslaved Africans. The ban, however, is widely ignored. Between 1808 and 1860, approximately 250,000 blacks are illegally imported into the United States. Slave trading within the states (the domestic trade) continues until the end of the Civil War.

1809 New York recognizes marriage within the African American community.

Abyssinian Baptist Church, destined to become by the 1930s the largest church in the United States, is founded in New York City.

1810 Census of 1810.
U.S. population: 7,239,881
Black population: 1,377,808 (19 percent) including 186,446 free African Americans.

The U.S. Congress prohibits African Americans from carrying mail for the U.S. Postal Service.

1811 Andry's Rebellion takes place in Louisiana on January 8–11. This servile insurrection, led by Charles Deslondes, formerly of Haiti, begins on the Louisiana plantation of Manuel Andry and spreads through the region between Baton Rouge and New Orleans.

1812 Previously independent African American schools become part of the Boston public school system.

Two African American regiments are formed in New York to fight in the War of 1812.

1813 Gradual emancipation is adopted in Argentina.

1815 Six hundred African American troops are among the three thousand of the U.S. Army, led by General Andrew Jackson, that defeats British forces at the Battle of New Orleans. The leader of the black troops, Joseph Savary, formerly of Haiti, is appointed major by Commanding General Andrew Jackson on December 19, 1814, and thus becomes the first African American officer in U.S. military history.

Gradual emancipation begins in Colombia.

Richard Allen presides over the organization of a number of independent AME churches and establishes the first wholly African American church denomination in the United States. It is called the African Methodist Episcopal (AME) Church.

Abolitionist Levi Coffin establishes the Underground Railroad.

1816 The American Colonization Society is founded by Bushrod Washington (the nephew of George Washington) and other prominent white Americans who believe enslaved African Americans should be freed and settled in Africa.

1817–18 Escaped slaves from Georgia, South Carolina, and Alabama join the military campaign of the Florida Seminoles to keep their homelands.

1818 Connecticut disenfranchises black male voters.

1819 The Canadian government refuses to cooperate with the American government in the apprehension of fugitive slaves living in Canada. Consequently Canada becomes the destination for forty thousand fugitive slaves from the United States between 1819 and 1861.

1820 Census of 1820.
U.S. population: 9,638,452
Black population: 1,771,656 (18.4 percent) including 233,504 free African Americans.

The Compromise of 1820 allows Missouri into the Union as a slave state and Maine as a free state. It also sets the boundary between slave and free territory in the West at the 36th parallel.

Reverend Daniel Coker of Baltimore leads eighty-six African Americans, who become the first black settlers to Liberia.

1821 New York maintains property qualifications for African American male voters while abolishing the same for white male voters. Missouri disenfranchises free black male voters.

On March 3, Thomas L. Jennings of New York City becomes the first African American to receive a patent from the U.S. Patent Office for an invention. Jennings, who owns a dry cleaning business in New York, develops a dry cleaning process called "dry scouring."

1822 Denmark Vesey is arrested for planning a slave rebellion in South Carolina.

Rhode Island disenfranchises black male voters.

Free blacks from the United States settle in Liberia under the auspices of the American Colonization Society.

1823 Slavery is abolished in Chile.

Alexander Twilight of Vermont becomes the first African American college graduate when he receives a degree from Middlebury College.

1824 Mexico outlaws slavery. This decision creates the incentive for Anglo Texans to fight for independence in 1835–36.

A white mob destroys most of the African American community of Providence, Rhode Island, ushering in a more than a century of white violence against northern black communities.

Slavery is abolished in Central America.

1827 *Freedom's Journal* begins publication on March 16 in New York City as the first African American–owned newspaper in the United States. The editors are John Russwurm and Samuel Cornish.

Slavery is officially abolished in New York.

1829 More than half of Cincinnati's African American residents are driven out of the city by white mob violence.

David Walker of Boston publishes *An Appeal to the Colored Citizens of the World,* which calls for a slave uprising in the South.

1830 Census of 1830.
U.S. population: 12,866,020
Black population: 2,328,842 (18.1 percent), including 319,599 free African Americans.

African American delegates from New York, Pennsylvania, Maryland, Delaware, and Virginia meet in Philadelphia in the first of a series of national Negro conventions to devise ways to challenge slavery in the South and racial discrimination in the North.

The American Society of Free People of Colour is organized in Philadelphia.

1831 North Carolina enacts a statute that bans teaching enslaved people to read and write.

Nat Turner leads a slave rebellion in Southampton, Virginia, killing at least fifty-seven whites. Hundreds of black slaves are killed in retaliation.

Alabama makes it illegal for enslaved or free blacks to preach.

William Lloyd Garrison of Boston founds *The Liberator,* the first abolitionist newspaper in the United States.

Slavery is abolished in Bolivia.

1832 Oberlin College is founded in Ohio. It admits African American men, black women, and white women. By 1860 one third of its students are black.

The Female Anti-Slavery Society, the first African American women's abolitionist society, is founded in Salem, Massachusetts.

1833 The American Anti-Slavery Society is established in Philadelphia.

The British Parliament abolishes slavery in the entire British Empire.

1834 African free schools are incorporated into the New York City public school system.

South Carolina bans the teaching of blacks, enslaved or free, in its borders.

1835 Texas declares its independence from Mexico. In its constitution as an independent nation, Texas recognizes slavery and makes it difficult for free blacks to remain there.

1836–44 The "Gag Rule" prohibits Congress from considering petitions regarding slavery.

1836 John B. Russwurm is appointed governor of the Cape Palmas district of Liberia by the American Colonization Society.

Alexander Twilight is elected to the Vermont Legislature from Orleans County. His election marks the first time an African American serves in a state legislature in the United States.

1837 The Institute for Colored Youth is founded in southeastern Pennsylvania. It later becomes Cheyney University.

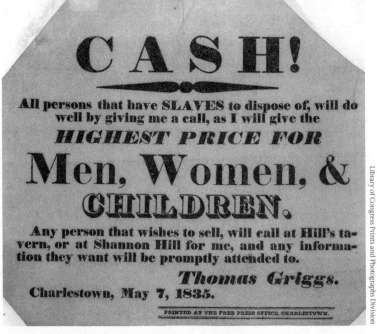

Advertisement for purchase of slaves by Thomas Griggs, Charlestown, 7 May 1835.

Dr. James McCune Smith of New York City graduates from the Medical School of the University of Glasgow and becomes the first African American to hold a medical degree.

1838 Pennsylvania disenfranchises black male voters.

1839 On August 29, American vessels tow the Spanish ship, the *Amistad,* and its fifty-three slaves into New London, Connecticut. Their fate is decided two years later by the U.S. Supreme Court.

1840 Census of 1840.
U.S. population: 17,069,453
Black population: 2,873,648 (16.1 percent), including 386,293 free African Americans.

1841 *The Christian Recorder,* the publication of the African Methodist Episcopal Church, appears for the first time in Philadelphia. The *Recorder* is the oldest continuously published African American periodical in the United States.

Great Britain, France, Russia, Prussia, and Austria mutually agree to the search of vessels on the high seas to suppress the slave trade.

On March 9, the U.S. Supreme Court rules in *United States v. The Amistad* that Africans on board the ship *Amistad* are free individuals who were kidnapped and illegally transported. Since they had never been slaves, they have the right to fight to defend their freedom. With that ruling, the Africans on the *Amistad* are allowed to return to their native lands.

In *Prigg v. Pennsylvania,* the U.S. Supreme Court rules that state officials are not required to capture fugitive slaves.

1842 Frederick Douglass leads a successful campaign against Rhode Island's proposed Dorr Constitution, which would have continued the prohibition on black male voting rights.

The Virginia Legislature votes against abolishing slavery.

Slavery is abolished in Uruguay.

1843 Reverend Henry Highland Garnet delivers his controversial "Address to the Slaves" at the National Negro Convention meeting in Buffalo, New York, which calls for a servile insurrection.

Sojourner Truth and William Wells Brown begin their campaigns against slavery.

1844 On June 25, the Legislative Committee of the Provisional Government of Oregon enacts the first of a series of black exclusion laws.

1845 Texas is annexed to the United States.

Frederick Douglass publishes his autobiography, *The Life and Times of Frederick Douglass.*

Macon Bolling Allen of Boston becomes the first African American licensed to practice law. Soon afterward he is appointed Justice of the Peace for Boston, becoming the first African American to hold judicial office.

1846–48 War with Mexico.

1847 Frederick Douglass, Martin Delaney, and William C. Nell begin publication of *The North Star* in Rochester, New York.

Missouri bans the education of free blacks.

Missouri abolitionists file a lawsuit on behalf of Dred Scott to gain his freedom. The case is decided by the U.S. Supreme Court a decade later.

Dr. David Jones Peck becomes the first African American to graduate from a U.S. medical school, Rush Medical College of Chicago.

Virginia slave Henry "Box" Brown escapes to freedom by climbing into a box for friends to ship him to Philadelphia.

Portrait of African American abolitionist and activist Frederick Douglass.

1848 On February 2, in the Treaty of Guadalupe Hidalgo, Mexico cedes California, Arizona, New Mexico, Nevada, and Utah, and gives up claim to Texas at the conclusion of the war in exchange for $20 million.

On July 19–20, Frederick Douglass is among the handful of men who attend the first Women's Rights Convention in Seneca Falls, New York.

Slavery is abolished in all French and Danish colonies.

1849 The California Gold Rush begins. Eventually four thousand African Americans migrate to California during this period.

Harriett Tubman escapes from slavery and begins her efforts to rescue enslaved people.

On December 4, Benjamin Roberts files a school desegregation lawsuit on behalf of his daughter, Sarah, who is denied admission to a Boston school. The lawsuit is unsuccessful.

Charles Lewis Reason becomes the first African American college instructor when he is hired at predominately white Free Mission College (later New York Central College) to teach Greek, Latin, French, and mathematics.

1850 Census of 1850.
U.S. population: 23,191,876
Black population: 3,638,808 (15.7 percent), including 433,807 free African Americans.

The Compromise of 1850 revisits the issue of slavery. California enters the Union as a free state, but the territories of New Mexico and Utah are allowed to decide whether they will enter the Union as slave or free states. The 1850 Compromise also allows passage of a much stricter Fugitive Slave Law.

On August 27, Lucy Stanton of Cleveland completes the course requirements for Oberlin Collegiate Institute (now Oberlin College) and becomes the first African American woman to graduate from an American college or university.

1851 Sojourner Truth delivers her famous "Aren't I a woman" speech at the Women's Rights Convention in Akron, Ohio, on May 29.

Slavery is abolished in Ecuador.

1852 Harriet Beecher Stowe publishes her novel, *Uncle Tom's Cabin,* which becomes a best-selling book and a major influence on the antislavery movement.

Harriet Jacobs, using the pen name Linda Brent, publishes her autobiography, *Incidents in the Life of a Slave Girl*. The volume is edited by white abolitionist Lydia Maria Child and receives wide attention as one of the most detailed accounts of slavery written by an enslaved person.

Martin R. Delany publishes *The Condition, Elevation, Emigration and Destiny of the Colored People of the United States,* which proposes the emigration of African Americans to Africa.

The Jackson Street Hospital in Augusta, Georgia, is established as the first medical facility solely for the care of African American patients.

1853 Elizabeth Taylor Greenfield (the Black Swan) debuts at the Metropolitan Opera in New York City and performs before Queen Victoria at Buckingham Palace a year later.

William Wells Brown becomes the first African American novelist when he publishes *Clotel, or the President's Daughter.*

1854 On May 24, Virginia fugitive slave Anthony Burns is captured in Boston and returned to slavery under the provisions of the Fugitive Slave Act. Fifty thousand Boston residents watch his transport through the streets of the city in shackles. A Boston church raises $1,500 to purchase his freedom and Burns returns to the city in 1855, a free man.

On May 30, the Kansas-Nebraska Act is passed by Congress. The act repeals the Missouri Compromise and permits the admission of Kansas and Nebraska territories to the Union after their white male voters decide the fate of slavery in those territories.

The Republican Party is formed in the summer in opposition to the extension of slavery into the western territories.

"Bleeding Kansas" is the most dramatic outgrowth of the controversy over the Kansas-Nebraska Act. Between 1854 and 1858 armed groups of pro- and antislavery factions often funded and sponsored by organizations in the North and South, compete for control of Kansas Territory, initiating waves of violence that kill fifty-five people. Bleeding Kansas is seen as a preview of the U.S. Civil War.

On October 13, Ashmun Institute, the first institution of higher learning for young black men, is founded by John Miller Dickey and his wife, Sarah Emlen Cresson. In 1866 it is renamed Lincoln University (Pa.) after President Abraham Lincoln.

James A. Healy is ordained in France as the first black Jesuit priest. In 1875 he becomes Bishop of Portland, Maine, a diocese that includes all of Maine and New Hampshire. Healy holds that post for twenty-five years.

Slavery is abolished in Peru and Venezuela.

1855 The Massachusetts Legislature outlaws racially segregated schools.

William C. Nell of Boston publishes *The Colored Patriots of the American Revolution,* considered the first history of African Americans.

In November, John Mercer Langston is elected town clerk of Brownhelm Township, Ohio, becoming the first black elected official in the United States.

1856 Wilberforce University becomes the first school of higher learning owned and operated by African Americans. It is founded by the African Methodist Episcopal Church. Bishop Daniel A. Payne becomes the institution's first president.

1857 On March 6, the Dred Scott decision is handed down by the U.S. Supreme Court. The ruling declares that enslaved people and their descendants can never be citizens and thus are not entitled to use the courts of the United States. It also rules that they are property protected by law in every state.

1858 Sarah Jane Woodson Early, who in 1856 was one of the first women graduates of Oberlin College, joins the faculty of Wilberforce College in Ohio. She is the first black woman to become a college professor.

Arkansas enslaves free black women and men who refuse to leave the state.

1859 Ten-year-old enslaved Thomas Greene "Blind Tom" Wiggins, a musical prodigy, plays classical music by Beethoven, Gottschalk, and Mozart before President James Buchanan in what is generally accepted as the first performance by an African American at the White House.

Harriett Wilson of Milford, New Hampshire, publishes *Our Nig; or Sketches from the Life of a Free Black,* the first novel by an African American woman.

On October 16, John Brown leads twenty men, including five African Americans, in an unsuccessful attempt to seize the Federal Armory at Harpers Ferry, Virginia, to inspire a slave insurrection.

1860 Census of 1860.
U.S. population: 31,443,321
Black population: 4,441,830 (14.1 percent), including 488,070 free African Americans.

On November 6, Abraham Lincoln is elected president.

On December 20, South Carolina secedes from the Union.

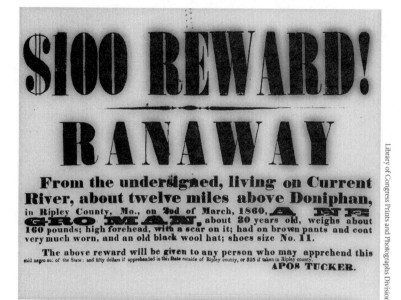

Escaped slave notice from Ripley County, Missouri, 1860.

1861–65 The Civil War. Approximately two hundred thousand blacks (most are newly escaped/freed slaves) serve in Union armed forces, and over twenty thousand are killed in combat.

1861 By February, Mississippi, Florida, Alabama, Georgia, Louisiana, and Texas secede. They form the Confederate States of America on March 4. After the firing on Fort Sumter near Charleston, South Carolina, on April 12, Virginia, Arkansas, Tennessee, and North Carolina secede.

The First Louisiana Native Guard, an all-black military regiment in New Orleans, joins the Confederate army shortly after the beginning of the Civil War. One year later, when the Confederates evacuate New Orleans, the Native Guard remains behind and joins the Union army as the Seventy-third Regiment Infantry, U.S. Colored Troops. Two other Native Guard regiments are also organized by black Louisiana residents.

1861 Congress passes the First Confiscation Act, which prevents Confederate slave owners from reenslaving runaways.

1862 The Port Royal (South Carolina) Reconstruction Experiment begins in March.

On April 16, Congress abolishes slavery in the District of Columbia.

In May, the coastal pilot Robert Smalls escapes Charleston, South Carolina, with *The Planter,* a Confederate vessel, along with sixteen enslaved people.

Congress permits the enlistment of African American soldiers in the U.S. Army on July 17.

With the Southern states absent from Congress, the body recognizes Haiti and Liberia, marking the first time diplomatic relations are established with predominately black nations.

Freedman's Hospital is established in Washington, D.C. It is the first federally funded health care facility for African Americans in the nation.

Born a slave in Georgia, Susie Baker (later Susie King Taylor) is the first African American U.S. Army nurse in the Civil War. She serves a regiment of black troops organized on the South Carolina coast.

Company E, 4th U.S. Colored Infantry, at Fort Lincoln in Washington, D.C., during the U.S. Civil War.

Library of Congress Prints and Photographs Division

1863 Abraham Lincoln's Emancipation Proclamation takes effect on January 1, legally freeing slaves in areas of the South still in rebellion against the United States.

On February 18, the Cherokee Emancipation Proclamation is issued by the Cherokee tribal government in Indian Territory. The Cherokee are the only Native American nation with enslaved black people to formally end the institution before 1865.

The New York City draft riots erupt on July 13 and continue for four days, during which at least one hundred of the city's residents are killed. This remains the highest death toll in any urban conflict in the nineteenth or twentieth century.

On July 18, the Fifty-Fourth Massachusetts Volunteers, the first officially recognized all-black military unit in the Union army, assaults Fort Wagner in Charleston, South Carolina, in an unsuccessful effort to take the fortification. Sergeant William H. Carney becomes the first African American to receive the Congressional Medal of Honor for bravery under fire.

Slavery is abolished in all Dutch colonies.

1864 The Fort Pillow Massacre takes place in West Tennessee on April 12. Approximately 300 of the 585 soldiers of the Union garrison at Fort Pillow are killed, including many after the Union forces surrender. Only 14 Confederate soldiers die in the battle.

In June, Dr. Rebecca Lee Crumpler of Boston is the first African American woman to earn a medical degree when she graduates from the New England Female Medical College in Boston.

On June 15, Congress passes a bill authorizing equal pay, equipment, arms, and health care for African American Union troops.

On October 4, the New Orleans *Tribune* begins publication. The *Tribune* is the first daily newspaper produced by African Americans.

1865 On February 1, Abraham Lincoln signs the Thirteenth Amendment to the U.S. Constitution outlawing slavery throughout the United States. With Georgia's ratification on December 6, the amendment becomes law.

Upon the order of President Abraham Lincoln, Martin Robinson Delany becomes the first African American commissioned at the rank of major in the regular infantry in the Civil War.

On March 3, Congress establishes the Freedmen's Bureau to provide health care, education, and technical assistance to emancipated slaves. Congress also charters the Freedman's Bank to promote savings and thrift among the ex-slaves.

Confederate general Robert E. Lee surrenders to Union general Ulysses S. Grant on April 9 at Appomattox Court House, Virginia, effectively ending the Civil War.

On April 15, President Abraham Lincoln is assassinated by John Wilkes Booth in Washington, D.C.

On June 19, enslaved African Americans in Texas finally receive news of their emancipation. A formal Emancipation Proclamation is issued on that day by Union general Gordon Granger after he and U.S. Army troops wade ashore at Galveston. From that point the people of Texas commemorate June 19 as "Juneteenth."

New Jersey–born John S. Rock, a physician, dentist, and teacher, and by 1861 a Boston attorney, becomes the first African American lawyer to argue a case before the U.S. Supreme Court.

Between September and November, a number of ex-Confederate states pass so-called Black Codes.

The Ku Klux Klan is formed on December 24 in Pulaski, Tennessee, by six educated, middle-class, Confederate veterans.

Twenty thousand African American troops are among the thirty-two thousand U.S. soldiers sent to the Rio Grande as a show of force against Emperor Maximilian's French troops occupying Mexico. Some discharged black soldiers join the forces of Mexican resistance leader Benito Juárez.

On November 21, Shaw University is founded in Raleigh, North Carolina.

1866 Fisk University is founded in Nashville, Tennessee, on January 9.

On April 9, Congress overrides President Andrew Johnson's veto to enact the Civil Rights Act of 1866. The act confers citizenship upon black Americans and guarantees equal rights with whites.

On May 1–3, white civilians and police in Memphis, Tennessee, kill forty-six African Americans and injure many more, burning ninety houses, twelve schools, and four churches in what becomes known as the Memphis Massacre.

On June 13, Congress approves the Fourteenth Amendment to the Constitution, guaranteeing due process and equal protection under the law to all citizens. The amendment also grants citizenship to African Americans.

Congress authorizes the creation of four all-black regiments in the U.S. Army. Two cavalry regiments, the Ninth and Tenth, and two infantry regiments, the Twenty-fourth and Twenty-fifth, become the first and only units in which black soldiers can serve (this is in effect until the Spanish-American War). They are known as Buffalo Soldiers.

Police in New Orleans supporting the Democratic mayor storm a Republican meeting of blacks and whites on July 30, killing 34 black and 3 white Republicans. Over 150 people are injured in the attack.

In November, Philadelphia-born Mifflin W. Gibbs is elected to the Victoria, British Columbia, City Council. Gibbs represents the city's wealthiest district and becomes the second black person to hold office in Canada (after Abraham D. Shadd, who was elected to the Raleigh, Ontario, Town Council in 1859) and only the third in North America after John Mercer Langston of Ohio.

1867 On January 8, Congress overrides President Andrew Johnson's veto and grants the black male citizens of the District of Columbia the right to vote. Two days later it passes the Territorial Suffrage Act, which allows African American men in the western territories to vote.

A chromolithograph of notable 19ᵗʰ century
African American men.

Morehouse College is founded in Atlanta on February 14.

The Reconstruction Acts are passed by Congress on March 2. Congress divides ten of the eleven ex-Confederate states into military districts. These acts also reorganize postwar Southern governments, disfranchising former high-ranking Confederates and enfranchising former slaves in the South.

On March 2, Howard University is chartered by Congress in Washington, D.C. The institution is named after General Oliver O. Howard, who heads the Freedman's Bureau.

Robert Tanner Freeman, born enslaved in North Carolina in 1847, is one of the first six graduates in dental medicine from Harvard University. He becomes the first African American to receive a dental degree from an American medical school.

1868 On July 21, with Georgia's ratification, the Fourteenth Amendment to the Constitution becomes law, granting citizenship to any person born or naturalized in the United States.

Opelousas, Louisiana, is the site of the Opelousas Massacre on September 28, in which an estimated two hundred to three hundred black Americans are killed by whites opposed to Reconstruction and African American voting.

On November 3, Civil War general Ulysses S. Grant (Republican) is elected President.

On November 3, Republican Oscar Dunn is elected lieutenant governor of Louisiana. At that point he is the highest-ranking elected black official in the nation.

On November 3, John Willis Menard is elected to Congress from Louisiana's Second Congressional District. Menard is the first African American elected to Congress. However, neither he nor his opponent is seated due to disputed election results.

Howard University Medical School opens on November 9.

1869 On February 26, Congress sends the Fifteenth Amendment to the Constitution to the states for approval. The amendment guarantees African American males the right to vote.

On April 6, Ebenezer Don Carlos Bassett is appointed minister to Haiti. He is the first black American diplomat and presidential appointee.

Mary Ann Shadd tries to register to vote in Washington, D.C. When she is turned away, she petitions Congress to extend the vote to women.

Isaac Myers organizes the Colored National Labor Union in Baltimore.

On December 10, Wyoming Territory extends voting rights to all women, including the eighty black women then living in the territory. They are the first black women to cast ballots, since New Jersey denied all women the right to vote in 1807.

1870 Census of 1870.
U.S. population: 39,818,449
Black population: 4,880,009 (12.7 percent)

Hiram R. Revels (Republican) of Mississippi takes his seat in the U.S. Senate on February 25. He is the first black U.S. senator, though he serves only one year, completing the unexpired term of Jefferson Davis.

The Fifteenth Amendment to the Constitution becomes law with Iowa's ratification on February 3.

In June, Richard T. Greener becomes the first African American to graduate from Harvard University.

In December, Robert H. Wood is elected mayor of Natchez, Mississippi. He is one of the earliest African American mayors in the nation.

1871 In February, Congress passes the Civil Rights Act of 1871, popularly known as the Ku Klux Klan Act.

On October 6, Fisk University's Jubilee Singers begin their first national tour. The Jubilee Singers become world-famous singers of black spirituals, performing before the Queen of England and the Emperor of Japan. The money they earn finances the construction of Jubilee Hall on the Fisk University campus.

1872 Charlotte Ray of Washington, D.C., becomes the first African American woman to practice law.

Lieutenant Governor Pinckney Benton Stewart Pinchback of Louisiana serves as governor of the state for one month, from December 1872 to January 1873. He is the first African American to hold that position.

1873 The Forty-third Congress has seven black members.

On April 14, the U.S Supreme Court in the Slaughterhouse Cases rules that the "due process" clause of the Fourteenth Amendment protects national, not state, citizenship.

Bishop Patrick Healy serves as president of Georgetown University from 1873 to 1881. He is the first African American to preside over a predominantly white university.

Slavery is abolished in Puerto Rico.

1874 The Freedman's Bank closes after African American depositors and investors lose more than $1 million.

1875 Federal troops are sent to Vicksburg, Mississippi, in January to protect African Americans attempting to vote and to allow the safe return of the African American sheriff who had been forced to flee the city.

On March 1, Congress enacts the Civil Rights Act of 1875, guaranteeing equal rights to black Americans in public accommodations and jury duty.

Blanche Kelso Bruce (Republican) of Mississippi becomes the first African American to serve a full six-year term as senator when Bruce takes his seat in the U.S. Senate on March 3.

The Forty-fourth Congress has eight black members.

On February 23, the first Southern "Jim Crow" laws are enacted in Tennessee. Similar statutes had existed in the North before the Civil War.

Five generations on Smith's Plantation, Beaufort, South Carolina
circa 1862.

1876 Lewis H. Latimer assists Alexander Graham
Bell in obtaining a patent for the telephone on
February 14.

In May, Edward Alexander Bouchet receives a Ph.D. from Yale University. He is the first African American to receive a Ph.D. from an American university and only the sixth American to earn a Ph.D. in physics. Bouchet is also believed to be the first African American elected to Phi Beta Kappa.

Race riots and other forms of terrorism against black voters in South Carolina over the summer prompt President Grant to send federal troops to restore order.

On October 13, Meharry Medical College is founded by the Freedman's Aid Society of the Methodist Church.

Harriett Purvis is elected the first black president of the American Woman Suffrage Association.

The presidential election of 1876, pitting Samuel Tilden (Democrat) against Rutherford B. Hayes (Republican), is inconclusive when the votes in the Electoral College are disputed.

1877 The Compromise of 1877 (also known as the Wormley House Compromise because the meeting takes place in a black-owned hotel in Washington, D.C.) is an arrangement worked out in January that effectively ends Reconstruction. Although Democratic presidential candidate Samuel Tilden won the popular vote, Southern Democratic leaders agree to support Rutherford Hayes's efforts to obtain the disputed electoral votes of Florida, Louisiana, and South Carolina in exchange for the withdrawal of the last federal troops from the South and the end of federal efforts to protect the civil rights of African Americans.

The Forty-fifth Congress has three black members.

On June 15, Henry O. Flipper of Atlanta, Georgia, becomes the first African American to graduate from West Point.

On July 30, African American settlers from Kentucky establish the town of Nicodemus in western Kansas. This is the first of hundreds of all-black or mostly black towns created in the West.

Frederick Douglass becomes U.S. Marshal for the District of Columbia.

1879–80 Approximately six thousand African Americans leave Louisiana and Mississippi counties along the Mississippi River for Kansas in what becomes known as the Exodus.

1879 Mary Eliza Mahoney becomes the first African American professionally trained nurse, graduating from the New England Hospital for Women and Children in Boston.

The Liberia Exodus Joint Stock Company sends the first post–Civil War African American emigrants to West Africa on the ship *Azor*.

1880 Census of 1880.
U.S. population: 50,155,783
Black population: 6,580,793 (13.1 percent)

In *Stauder v. West Virginia*, the United States Supreme Court rules that excluding African Americans from juries is unconstitutional.

On May 14, Sergeant George Jordan of the Ninth Cavalry, commanding a detachment of Buffalo Soldiers, leads a successful defense of Tularosa, New Mexico Territory, against Apache Indians.

1881 In January, the Tennessee State Legislature votes to segregate railroad passenger cars. Tennessee's action is followed by Florida (1887), Mississippi (1888), Texas (1889), Louisiana (1890), Alabama, Kentucky, Arkansas, and Georgia (1891), South Carolina (1898), North Carolina (1899), Virginia (1900), Maryland (1904), and Oklahoma (1907).

Spelman College (originally the Atlanta Baptist Female Seminary) becomes the first college for black women in the United States. It is founded on April 11 by two white teachers from Worcester, Massachusetts, Sophia B. Packard and Harriet E. Giles. Later that year the seminary establishes the first school for black nurses. The institution is renamed Spelman Seminary after Laura Spelman Rockefeller, the wife of early benefactor John D. Rockefeller.

On the Fourth of July, Booker T. Washington opens Tuskegee Institute in central Alabama.

The signature of Blanche K. Bruce, former U.S. senator from Mississippi and now Register of the Treasury, appears on all U.S. paper currency.

1883 On January 13, former slaves found the Richmond *Planet* in Richmond, Virginia. Edited between 1884 and 1929 by John Mitchell, Jr., it becomes one of the most successful papers of its era.

The Fiftieth Congress has no black members. Intimidation keeps most black voters from the polls.

On October 16, the U.S. Supreme Court declares invalid the Civil Rights Act of 1875, stating the federal government cannot bar corporations or individuals from discriminating on the basis of race.

On November 3, white conservatives in Danville, Virginia, seize control of the local racially integrated and popularly elected government, killing four African Americans in the process.

1884 Christopher J. Perry establishes the Philadelphia *Tribune,* the longest continuously operating African American newspaper in the nation.

On May 1, Moses Fleetwood Walker becomes the first black professional baseball player when he debuts as a catcher with the Toledo Blue Stockings in a game against the Louisville Eclipse.

1885 On June 25, African American Samuel David Ferguson is ordained as the first African American bishop of the Episcopal Church.

Chicago furniture store owner and former slave Sarah E. Goode develops a hideaway bed that folds into a cabinet that also serves as a rolltop desk. The bed-and-desk combination proves popular among the residents of the city's small apartments, prompting Goode to apply for a U.S. patent, which is awarded on July 14.

1886 Slavery is abolished in Cuba.

The Knights of Labor reaches it peak membership of seven hundred thousand with approximately seventy-five thousand African American members.

The American Federation of Labor is organized on December 8. All major unions of the federation exclude black workers.

1887 African American players are banned from major league baseball.

The National Colored Farmers' Alliance is formed in Houston County, Texas.

1888 On April 11, Edward Park Duplex is elected mayor of Wheatland, California. He is believed to be the first African American mayor of a predominantly white town in the United States.

Two of America's first black-owned banks, the Savings Bank of the Grand Fountain United Order of the Reformers, in Richmond, Virginia, and Capital Savings Bank of Washington, D.C., open their doors.

Slavery is abolished in Brazil.

1889 Florida becomes the first state to use the poll tax to disenfranchise black voters.

Frederick Douglass is appointed minister to Haiti.

U.S. Army officer Augustus Boutelle Frazier is appointed superintendent of Yellowstone National Park. He holds the post for one year.

1890 Census of 1890.
U.S. population: 62,947,714
Black population: 7,488,676 (11.9 percent)

The Afro-American League is founded on January 25 in Chicago under the leadership of Timothy Thomas Fortune, editor of the New York *Age*.

On November 1, the Mississippi Legislature approves a new state constitution that disenfranchises virtually all of the state's African American voters. The Mississippi Plan uses literacy and "understanding" tests to prevent African Americans from casting ballots. Similar statutes are adopted by South Carolina (1895), Louisiana (1898), North Carolina (1900), Alabama (1901), Virginia (1901), Georgia (1908), and Oklahoma (1910).

1891 Dr. Daniel Hale Williams founds Provident Hospital in Chicago, the first African American–owned hospital in the nation. Provident is also one of the first interracial hospitals.

1892 In June, soprano Matilda Sissieretta Jones becomes the first African American to perform at Carnegie Hall. Earlier in the year she performed at the White House for President Benjamin Harrison and at Madison Square Garden. Jones is the most well-known and highest-paid black performer of the era.

On July 14, three companies of the Twenty-fifth Infantry occupy the Coeur d'Alene Mining District in northern Idaho, which has been under martial law following a violent strike by silver miners. The infantry remains for four months.

A record 230 people are lynched in the United States this year; 161 are black and 69 white. In the period between 1882 and 1951, Tuskegee Institute compiles nationwide lynching statistics. In that sixty-nine-year period, 4,730 people are lynched, including 3,437 blacks and 1,293 whites. Ninety-two women are victims of lynching: 76 are black and 16 are white. Although southern states accounted for 90 percent of the lynchings, every state in the continental United States, with the exception of Massachusetts, Rhode Island, New Hampshire, and Vermont, report lynching deaths sometime during the sixty-nine-year period.

In October, activist Ida B. Wells begins her antilynching campaign with the publication of *Southern Horrors: Lynch Law in All Its Phases* and a speech in New York City's Lyric Hall.

The National Medical Association is formed in Atlanta by African American physicians because they are barred from the American Medical Association.

The first intercollegiate football game between African American colleges takes place between Biddle University (now Johnson C. Smith University) and Livingston College on December 27 on a snow-covered field in Charlotte, North Carolina. Biddle University wins the contest, 4–0.

1893 Henry Ossawa Tanner paints *The Banjo Lesson,* which is eventually hailed as one of the major works of art of the late nineteenth century.

Dr. Daniel Hale Williams performs the first successful operation on a human heart. The patient, a victim of a chest stab wound, survives and lives for twenty years after the operation.

1895 White terrorists attack black workers in New Orleans on March 11–12. Six blacks are killed.

In June, W. E. B. Du Bois becomes the first African American to receive a Ph.D. from Harvard University.

Booker T. Washington delivers his famous "Atlanta Compromise" address on September 18 at the Atlanta Cotton States Exposition. He says the "Negro problem" would be solved by a policy of gradualism and accommodation.

Three black Baptist organizations—the Foreign Mission Baptist Convention of the United States (1880), the American National Baptist Convention (1886), and the Baptist National Educational Convention (1893)—combine at Friendship Baptist Church in Atlanta to form the National Baptist Convention of America, Inc. The National Baptist Convention is the largest black religious denomination in the United States.

Dr. Nathan Francis Mossell of Philadelphia founds the Frederick Douglass Memorial Hospital and Training School for Nurses.

1896 *Plessey v. Ferguson* is decided on May 18 when the United States Supreme Court rules that Southern segregation laws and practices (Jim Crow) do not conflict with the Thirteenth and Fourteenth Amendments. The Court defends its ruling by articulating the "separate but equal" doctrine.

On July 21, the National Association of Colored Women is formed in Washington, D.C. Mary Church Terrell is chosen as its first president.

In September, George Washington Carver is appointed director of agricultural research at Tuskegee Institute. His work advances peanut, sweet potato, and soybean farming.

1897 The American Negro Academy is established on March 5 in Washington, D.C., to encourage African American participation in art, literature, and philosophy.

The first Phillis Wheatley Home is founded in Detroit. These homes, established in most cities with large African American populations, provide temporary accommodations and social services for single African American women.

President William McKinley appoints Richard R. Wright as the first African American U.S. Army paymaster. Wright also serves as president of the Georgia State Industrial College for Colored Youth (1891–1921) and in 1921, at the age of sixty-seven, he moves to Philadelphia and opens the first African American–owned bank in a Northern city.

1898 In January, the Louisiana Legislature introduces the "Grandfather Clause" into the state's constitution. Only males whose fathers or grandfathers were qualified to vote on January 1, 1867, are automatically registered. Others (African Americans) must comply with educational or property requirements.

The Spanish-American War begins on April 21. Sixteen regiments of black volunteers are recruited; four see combat in Cuba and the Philippines. Five African Americans win Congressional Medals of Honor during the war. A number of black officers command troops for the first time.

The United States Supreme Court, in *Williams v. Mississippi*, rules that poll taxes and literacy tests do not violate the Constitution.

The National Afro-American Council is founded on September 15 in Washington, D.C. The organization elects Bishop Alexander Walters as its first president.

On November 10, in Wilmington, North Carolina, eight black Americans are killed during white rioting as conservative Democrats drive out of power black and white Republican officeholders in the city.

The North Carolina Mutual and Provident Insurance Company of Durham, North Carolina, and the National Benefit Life Insurance Company of Washington, D.C., are established.

1899 In May, units of the Twenty-fourth Infantry occupy the Coeur d'Alene Mining District in northern Idaho after violence again erupts.

The Afro-American Council designates June 4 as a national day of fasting to protest lynching and massacres.

1900 Census of 1900.
U.S. population: 75,994,575
Black population: 8,833,994 (11.6 percent)

In January, James Weldon Johnson writes the lyrics and his brother John Rosamond Johnson composes the music for *Lift Every Voice and Sing* in their hometown of Jacksonville, Florida, in celebration of the birthday of Abraham Lincoln. The song is eventually adopted as the black national anthem.

The United States Pavilion at the Paris Exposition (April 14–November 10) houses an exhibition on black Americans called the Exposition des Negres d'Amérique.

The first Pan-African Conference, organized by Henry Sylvester Williams, a Trinidad attorney, meets in London in July.

The New Orleans Race Riot (also known as the Robert Charles Riot) erupts on July 23 and lasts four days. Twelve African Americans and seven whites are killed.

On August 23, the National Negro Business League is founded in Boston by Booker T. Washington to promote business enterprise.

In September, Nannie Helen Burroughs leads the founding of the Women's Convention of the National Baptist Convention at its meeting in Richmond, Virginia.

The Washington Society of Colored Dentists is founded in Washington, D.C. It is the first African American association of dentists.

This year marks the beginning of significant West Indian immigration to the United States.

Booker T. Washington publishes *Up from Slavery*, his autobiography.

Worker in an Alabama chemical plant
in 1942.

CHAPTER FIVE

THE AFRICAN AMERICAN CENTURY

Timeline: 1901–2000

The twentieth century was in many ways the turning point in the African American struggle for justice and advancement in American society. When the century began, approximately 90 percent of nearly nine million African Americans resided in the rural areas of the American South. Most were poor and disenfranchised. They suffered under oppressive economic and political conditions hardly better than during the days of slavery.

By the end of the century, legal racial segregation and discrimination had been outlawed. With the rise of a substantial middle class, most African Americans were no longer poor. They lived in all sections of the nation and served in capacities in the public and private sectors that would have been unimaginable in 1901.

While there are numerous factors that generated this sweeping transformation, three overarching but related ones stand out. The first was the migration of millions of black folks from the rural South and, to a lesser extent, from the West Indies, to the urban North. That unprecedented migration began in the second decade of the century and continued through the 1970s.

Relatedly, the political protest spirit as reflected in the World War II "Double Victory" Campaign and the March on Washington movement, combined with labor shortages, brought millions of African Americans into industrial jobs in the 1940s, which in turn lifted hundreds of thousands out of poverty.

The growing confidence stemming from both prosperity and the ability to successfully organize to demand racial justice in the 1940s contributed to the third factor, the civil rights-black power movement in the 1950s and 1960s. Those movements, which produced remarkable leaders, such as Martin Luther King, Jr., Rosa Parks, and Malcolm X, also energized tens of thousands of "ordinary" black people throughout the country to do whatever was necessary to end poverty and discrimination. The stunning achievements of these well-known and unheralded activists forced the United States government and millions of its non-black citizens to finally confront the centuries-old contradiction between the proclaiming of democracy and its denial in practice. While this transformation was stalled by the resurgence of conservative American politics in the 1980s, the twentieth century was, to borrow a phrase from scholars Henry Louis Gates and Cornel West, the "African-American Century" in that black folks, as never before, became central figures in the political, cultural, and economic life of the nation.

TIMELINE
1901–2000

1901 The last African American congressman elected in the nineteenth century, George H. White, Republican of North Carolina, leaves office. No African American will serve in Congress for the next twenty-eight years.

On October 11, Bert Williams and George Walker record their music for the Victor Talking Machine Company, becoming the first African American recording artists.

On October 16, only one month after becoming president, Theodore Roosevelt holds an afternoon meeting at the White House with Booker T. Washington. At the end of the meeting, the president informally invites Washington to remain for dinner, making the Tuskegee educator the first black American to dine at the White House with a president. Roosevelt's casual act generates a national furor over what many called his inadvertent promotion of racial equality.

1902 In May, jockey Jimmy Winkfield wins the Kentucky Derby in an era when African American jockeys dominate the sport.

Harry "Bucky" Lew becomes the first professional African American basketball player when he joins Lowell, Massachusetts's Pawtucketville Athletic Club, which was then part of the New England Professional Basketball League.

1903 W. E. B. Du Bois's *The Souls of Black Folk* is published on April 27. In it Du Bois rejects the gradualism of Booker T. Washington, calling for agitation on behalf of African American rights.

Maggie Lena Walker founds St. Luke's Penny Savings Bank in Richmond, Virginia, becoming the first African American woman bank president.

Meta Vaux Warrick, an African American sculptor, exhibits her work at the Paris Salon, in Paris, France.

1904 Educator Mary McLeod Bethune founds a college in Daytona Beach, Florida, that today is known as Bethune–Cookman College.

Sigma Pi Beta (the Boule) is founded in Philadelphia by four wealthy black professionals. The Boule is the first African American fraternity exclusively for college graduates.

Dr. Solomon Carter Fuller, who trains at the Royal Psychiatric Hospital at the University of Munich with Dr. Alois Alzheimer, becomes a widely published pioneer in Alzheimer's disease research. Fuller also becomes the nation's first black psychiatrist.

Charles W. Follis becomes the first African American professional football player when he joins the Shelby Athletic Association in Shelby, Ohio.

1905 The Chicago *Defender* is founded by Robert Abbott on May 5.

The Niagara Movement, an early civil rights organization, is created on July 11–13 by African American intellectuals and activists, led by W. E. B. Du Bois and William Monroe Trotter.

Nashville African Americans boycott streetcars to protest racial segregation.

Alonzo Herndon founds the Atlanta Life Insurance Company.

1906 The Azusa Street Revival begins in the former African Methodist Episcopal Church building at 312 Azusa Street in Los Angeles in April. The revival, led by black evangelist William J. Seymour, is considered the beginning of the worldwide Pentecostal movement.

On August 13, in Brownsville, Texas, approximately a dozen black troops riot against segregation and in the process kill a local citizen. When the identity of the killer cannot be determined, President Theodore Roosevelt discharges three companies of black soldiers on November 6.

A race riot in Atlanta on September 22–24 produces twelve deaths, ten blacks and two whites.

On December 4, seven students at Cornell University form Alpha Phi Alpha Fraternity, the first of eight major fraternities and sororities formed by black collegians.

1907 Alain Locke of Philadelphia, a Harvard graduate, becomes the first African American Rhodes Scholar to study at Oxford University in England.

The Pittsburgh *Courier* is established by Edwin Harleston, a security guard and aspiring writer. Three years later attorney Robert Vann takes control of the paper as its editor-publisher.

While living in Denver, Madame C. J. Walker develops and markets her hair-straightening method and creates one of the most successful cosmetics firms in the nation.

1908 On January 15, Alpha Kappa Alpha, the first black sorority, is founded on the campus of Howard University.

John Baxter "Doc" Taylor of the University of Pennsylvania becomes the first African American to win an Olympic Gold Medal. His event is the 400-meter medley at the London games.

On August 14, a two-day race riot breaks out in Springfield, Illinois, the hometown of Abraham Lincoln. Two blacks and four whites are killed. This is the first major riot in a Northern city in nearly half a century.

1909 The National Association for the Advancement of Colored People (NAACP) is formed on February 12 in New York City, partly in response to the Springfield Riot.

On April 6, Admiral Robert E. Peary and African American explorer Matthew Henson, accompanied by four Eskimos, become the first men known to have reached the North Pole.

W. E. B. Du Bois proposes the *Encyclopedia Africana,* a compilation of the vast array of knowledge about Africa and African America.

On December 4, the *Amsterdam News* begins publication and quickly becomes the major black newspaper in New York City and one of the largest in the nation.

1910 Census of 1910.
U.S. population: 93,402,151
Black population: 9,827,763 (10.7 percent)

The National Urban League is founded
in New York City on September 23.
The league is organized to help African
Americans secure employment and to
adjust to urban life.

On July 4, boxer Jack Johnson defeats
Jim Jeffries in Reno, Nevada, to become
the first African American world heavyweight
champion.

The first issue of *Crisis,* the official publication
of the NAACP, appears on November 1.
W. E. B. Du Bois is the first editor.

On December 19, the City Council
of Baltimore approves an ordinance
segregating black and white neighborhoods.
This ordinance is followed by similar
statutes in Dallas, Texas; Greensboro,
North Carolina; Louisville, Kentucky;
Norfolk, Virginia; Oklahoma City,
Oklahoma; Richmond, Virginia;
Roanoke, Virginia; and St. Louis,
Missouri.

Boxer Jack Johnson,
first African American heavyweight champion,
in 1915.

1911 Kappa Alpha Psi fraternity, the second
fraternity for black college students, is founded
at Indiana University on January 5.

Arturo Schomburg and Edward Bruce cofound
the Negro Society for Historical Research.

Scott Joplin completes his folk opera, *Treemonisha*,
which is later staged in 1915.

Andrew "Rube" Foster creates the Chicago
American Giants, the first of the major teams in
the Negro Baseball League.

Omega Psi Phi fraternity, the third black college fraternity, is founded at Howard University on November 17.

1913 The jubilee year, the fiftieth anniversary of the Emancipation Proclamation, is celebrated throughout the nation over the entire year.

Delta Sigma Theta sorority, the second black college sorority, is founded at Howard University on January 13.

On April 11, President Woodrow Wilson initiates the racial segregation of workplaces, restrooms, and lunchrooms in all federal offices across the nation.

Southern University is established in Baton Rouge, Louisiana.

1914 Phi Beta Sigma fraternity, the fourth black college fraternity, is founded at Howard University on January 9.

The Universal Negro Improvement Association (UNIA) is founded in Kingston, Jamaica, by Marcus and Amy Jacques Garvey.

Cleveland inventor Garrett Morgan patents a gas mask called the Safety Hood and Smoke Protector. The mask, initially used to rescue trapped miners, is eventually adopted by the U.S. Army.

On August 1, World War I begins in Europe.

African American pilot Eugene J. Bullard volunteers to serve with the French Air Force in World War I. He is the first black pilot to see combat in that conflict.

Bert Williams plays the lead role in *Darktown Jubilee,* making him the first African American actor to star in a motion picture.

1915 The Great Migration of African Americans from the South to Northern cities begins.

On June 21, the Oklahoma Grandfather Clause is overturned in *Guinn v. United States.*

On July 28, the United States begins a nineteen-year occupation of Haiti, the longest occupation in U.S. history.

In September, Carter G. Woodson founds the Association for the Study of Negro Life and History in Chicago. The association produces *The Journal of Negro History* the following year.

Dr. Ernest E. Just wins the Spingarn Medal, the highest award of the NAACP, for his pioneering research on fertilization and cell division.

Ferdinand Joseph La Menthe "Jelly Roll" Morton publishes *The "Jelly Roll" Blues*.

1916 Marcus Garvey founds the New York Division of the Universal Negro Improvement Association with sixteen members. Four years later the UNIA holds its national convention in Harlem. At its height, the organization claims nearly two million members.

In March, the Tenth Cavalry is one of two cavalry units under the command of General John J. Pershing given the assignment to capture Mexican Revolutionary leader Pancho Villa. The Seventh Cavalry is the other. They are unsuccessful.

On July 25, Garrett Morgan uses his newly invented gas mask to rescue thirty-two men trapped after an explosion in a tunnel 250 feet beneath Lake Erie.

1917 The United States enters World War I on April 6. Over 370,000 African Americans join the armed forces with more than half serving in the French war zone. Over 1,000 black officers command these troops. The French government awards the Croix de Guerre to 107 African American soldiers.

The East St. Louis Race Riot begins on July 1 and continues to July 3. Forty people are killed, hundreds more injured, and six thousand driven from their homes.

Nearly ten thousand African Americans and their supporters march down Manhattan's Fifth Avenue on July 28 as part of a "silent parade," an NAACP-organized protest against lynchings, race riots, and the denial of rights. This is the first major civil rights demonstration in the twentieth century.

On August 23, a riot erupts in Houston between black soldiers and white citizens; two blacks and eleven whites are killed. Twenty-nine black soldiers are executed for participation in the riot.

Lucy Diggs Slowe wins the championship in the first national tennis tournament sponsored by the American Tennis Association. With her victory she becomes the first African American woman to win a major sports title. Slowe was also one of the founders of the Alpha Kappa Alpha sorority (1908) and the first dean of women at Howard University (1922).

In August, A. Philip Randolph and Chandler Owen found *The Messenger,* a black socialist magazine, in New York City.

On November 5, the Supreme Court in *Buchanan v. Warley* strikes down the Louisville,

Kentucky, ordinance mandating segregated neighborhoods.

1918 On July 25–28, a race riot in Chester, Pennsylvania, claims five lives, those of three blacks and two whites.

On July 26–29, in nearby Philadelphia, another race riot breaks out, killing four, three blacks and one white.

The Armistice on November 11 ends World War I. However, the northern migration of African Americans continues. By 1930 there are 1,035,000 more black Americans in the North than in 1910.

1919 The Ku Klux Klan is revived in 1915 at Stone Mountain, Georgia, and by the beginning of 1919 it operates in twenty-seven states. Eighty-three African Americans are lynched during the year, among them a number of returning soldiers still in uniform.

The West Virginia State Supreme Court rules that an African American is denied equal protection under the law if his jury has no black members.

The Second Pan-African Conference, led by W. E. B. Du Bois, meets in Paris in February, partly to help influence the postwar Versailles peace conference.

The Associated Negro Press is established by
Claude A. Barnett on March 2.

The twenty-five race riots that take place
throughout the nation prompt the term
"Red Summer." The largest clashes take place
on May 10 in Charleston, South Carolina;
July 13 in Longview, Texas; July 19–23 in
Washington, D.C.; July 27–Aug. 1 in Chicago;
September 28 in Omaha; and October 1–3 in
Elaine, Arkansas.

Claude McKay publishes the poem "If We
Must Die," considered one of the first major
examples of Harlem Renaissance writing.

Father Divine founds the Peace Mission
movement at his home in Sayville,
New York.

Frederick Douglass "Fritz" Pollard becomes
the first African American football player in
the National Football League when he joins
the Akron Pros as a running back. Two years
later he becomes player-coach of the team.

South Dakota resident Oscar Micheaux
releases his first film, *The Homesteader,*
in Chicago. Over the next four decades
Micheaux produces and directs twenty-four
silent films and nineteen sound films,
making him the most prolific black
filmmaker of the twentieth century.

1920 Census of 1920.
U.S. population: 105,710,620
Black population: 10,463,131 (9.9 percent)

The decade of the 1920s witnesses the Harlem Renaissance, a remarkable period of creativity for dozens of black writers, poets, and artists, including, among others, Claude McKay, Jean Toomer, Langston Hughes, and Zora Neale Hurston.

On January 16, Zeta Phi Beta sorority, the third black sorority, is founded at Howard University.

Andrew "Rube" Foster leads the effort to establish the Negro National (Baseball) League on February 14 in Kansas City. Eight teams are part of the league.

On August 26, the Nineteenth Amendment to the Constitution is ratified, giving all women the right to vote. Nonetheless, African American women, like African American men, are denied the franchise in most Southern states.

1921 On May 31–June 1, at least sixty blacks and twenty-one whites are killed in a race riot in Tulsa, Oklahoma. The violence destroys a thriving African American neighborhood and business district called Deep Greenwood.

In June, Sadie Tanner Mossell Alexander of the University of Pennsylvania, Eva B. Dykes of Radcliffe, and Georgiana R. Simpson of the University of Chicago become the first African American women to earn Ph.D. degrees.

Bessie Coleman, the first black female pilot, becomes the first woman to receive an international pilot's license when she graduates from the Fédération Aéronautique International in France.

Harry Pace forms Black Swan Phonograph Corporation, the first African American–owned record company in the United States. His artists will include Mamie and Bessie Smith.

One of the earliest exhibitions of work by African American artists, including Henry Ossawa Tanner and Meta Vaux Warrick Fuller, is held at the 135th Street branch of the New York Public Library. This is one of the earliest events signaling the rise of the Harlem Renaissance.

Dr. Meta L. Christy, a graduate of the Philadelphia College of Osteopathic Medicine, becomes the nation's first osteopathic physician.

1922 *Shuffle Along* by Noble Sissle and Eubie Blake opens on Broadway on May 23. This is the first major theatrical performance of the Harlem Renaissance.

In September, William Leo Hansberry of Howard University teaches the first course in African history and civilization at an American university.

Sigma Gamma Rho sorority, the last of the four major black college fraternities and sororities, is founded on November 12 in Indianapolis, Indiana.

The Harmon Foundation is established in New York City to promote African American participation in the fine arts.

The Dyer Anti-Lynching Bill, making lynching a federal offense and first introduced by St. Louis congressman Leonidas Dyer in 1918, passes the U.S. House of Representatives but fails in the U.S. Senate.

1923 On January 4, the small, predominantly black town of Rosewood, Florida, is destroyed by a mob of white residents from nearby communities.

Marcus Garvey is imprisoned for mail fraud. He is sent to the federal penitentiary in Atlanta in 1925.

In September, the Cotton Club opens in Harlem.

Bessie Smith signs with Columbia Records to produce "race" records. Two years later she records "St. Louis Blues" with Louis Armstrong.

On November 20, Garrett T. Morgan patents the traffic signal.

The National Urban League publishes its first issue of *Opportunity, A Journal of Negro Life*. The magazine, edited by Charles S. Johnson, quickly becomes a forum for artists and authors of the Harlem Renaissance.

1924 Eugene O'Neill's play *The Emperor Jones* opens in London, with Paul Robeson in the title role.

Photographer James Vander Zee begins his career by capturing images of Marcus Garvey and the UNIA.

William DeHart Hubbard becomes the first African American to win an individual Olympic Gold Medal. He is the champion of the long jump at the 1924 Summer Olympics in Paris.

1925 Alain Locke's *The New Negro* is published in New York City. His anthology becomes the major contemporary work profiling the Harlem Renaissance.

The National Bar Association, an organization of black attorneys, is established on August 1 in Des Moines, Iowa.

On August 2, the Brotherhood of Sleeping Car Porters and Maids is organized, with A. Philip Randolph as its first president.

An all-white New Rochelle, New York, jury finds in favor of Alice Jones in *Rhinelander v. Jones* in their famous divorce case. Leonard Kip Rhinelander demands an annulment because Jones deceived him by claiming she was white. Jones's attorneys successfully argue that Jones, although light-skinned, was known as "colored." Despite the ruling, the couple never again lived together and legally separated in 1930.

Clifton R. Wharton, Sr., becomes the first African American foreign service officer.

On September 9, Ossian Sweet, a Detroit physician, is arrested for murder after he and his family kill a member of a white mob while defending their home. The Sweet family is represented at their trial by Clarence Darrow, and they are acquitted of the charge.

1926 Carter G. Woodson establishes Negro History Week in February between the birthdays of Lincoln and Washington.

Dr. Mordecai Johnson becomes the first African American president of Howard University in September.

The Carnegie Corporation purchases Arturo Schomburg's collection of books and artifacts on African American life. The collection becomes the basis for the Schomburg Center for Research in Black Culture in New York City.

A group of black women are beaten by election officials when they attempt to register to vote in Birmingham, Alabama.

1927 Twenty-four-year-old Chicago businessman Abe Saperstein forms the Harlem Globetrotters basketball team on January 30. The team was created in Illinois and was originally known as the Savoy Big Five.

In *Gong Lum v. Rice,* the United States Supreme Court rules that the Mississippi Chinese can be classified as "black" and thus restricted to segregated schools.

On December 2, Marcus Garvey is deported from the United States.

Dr. William Augustus Hinton develops the Hinton test for diagnosing syphilis. In 1936 his book, *Syphilis and Its Treatment,* becomes the first medical textbook written by an African American to be published.

1928 On November 6, Oscar DePriest, a Republican, is elected to Congress from Chicago's South Side. He is the first African American to represent a Northern, urban district.

The Atlanta *Daily World* begins publication in November.

The Apollo Theater opens in Harlem.

1929 Fats Waller's *Ain't Misbehavin'* opens on Broadway.

20th Annual session of the N.A.A.C.P. in Cleveland, Ohio in 1929.

1930 Census of 1930.
U.S. population: 122,775,046
Black population: 11,891,143 (9.7 percent)

James V. Herring establishes the Howard University Gallery of Art, the first gallery in the United States directed and controlled by African Americans. It is also one of the earliest galleries to highlight African American art.

Wallace Fard Muhammad founds the Nation of Islam in Detroit in 1930. Four years later Elijah Muhammad assumes control over the organization and transfers the headquarters to Chicago.

1931 Walter White is named NAACP executive secretary. Soon afterward the NAACP mounts a new strategy primarily using lawsuits to end racial discrimination.

The Scottsboro Boys are arrested in Alabama. Their trial begins on April 6.

1932 The Tuskegee Syphilis Experiment begins under the direction of the U.S. Public Health Service. The experiment ends in 1972.

Gospel composer Thomas Dorsey writes "Take My Hand, Precious Lord."

Franklin Delano Roosevelt is elected President of the United States in November.

The United States Supreme Court, in *Powell v. Alabama,* rules that the Scottsboro defendants must be retried because Alabama officials violated the Fourteenth Amendment by denying them adequate legal counsel.

The Los Angeles *Sentinel* is founded by Leon H. Washington.

Dudley Murphy releases the film *The Emperor Jones* starring Paul Robeson.

1934 W. E. B. Du Bois resigns from the NAACP in a dispute over the strategy of the organization in its campaign against racial discrimination. Roy Wilkins becomes the new editor of *Crisis* magazine.

The Southern Tenant Farmers Union is organized in Arkansas by the Socialist Party.

In *Herndon v. Georgia,* the U.S. Supreme Court sets aside the death sentence of black Communist Angelo Herndon, who was convicted under a pre–Civil War slave insurrection statute for passing out leaflets in Atlanta.

Zora Neale Hurston's first novel, *Jonah's Gourd Vine,* is published.

1935 On March 20, a one-day riot erupts in Harlem, leaving two people dead.

On April 1, the U.S. Supreme Court rules in *Norris v. Alabama* that a defendant has a right to trial by a jury of his or her peers.

The Michigan *Chronicle* is founded in Detroit by Louis E. Martin.

On October 3, Italy invades Ethiopia.

On November 5, the Maryland Supreme Court rules in *Murray v. Pearson* that the University of Maryland must admit African Americans to its law school or establish a separate school for blacks. The University of Maryland chooses to admit its first black students.

On December 24, Mary McLeod Bethune calls together the leaders of twenty-eight national women's organizations to Washington, D.C., to found the National Council of Negro Women.

1936 The first meeting of the National Negro Congress takes place in Chicago on February 14, 1936. Nearly six hundred black organizations are represented.

On June 24, Mary McLeod Bethune is named director of the Division of Negro Affairs, the National Youth Administration. She is the highest-ranking black official in the Roosevelt administration and leads the "Black Cabinet," an informal group of high-ranking African American appointees in the Roosevelt administration. Bethune is also the first black woman to receive a presidential appointment.

Track star Jesse Owens wins four Gold Medals at the Berlin Olympics between August 3 and August 9.

William Grant Still becomes the first African American to conduct a major U.S. orchestra, the Los Angeles Philharmonic.

1937 William H. Hastie, former adviser to President Franklin Roosevelt, is confirmed on March 26 as the first black federal judge after his appointment by Roosevelt to the federal bench in the Virgin Islands.

The Brotherhood of Sleeping Car Porters and Maids is recognized by the Pullman Company.

Approximately eighty African Americans are among the three thousand U.S. volunteers who fight in the Spanish Civil War. One of them, Oliver Law of Chicago, commands the Lincoln Battalion. Law is killed in battle on July 9.

On June 22, boxer Joe Louis wins the World Heavyweight Championship in a bout with James J. Braddock in Chicago.

In October, Katherine Dunham forms the Negro Dance Group, a company of black artists dedicated to presenting aspects of African American and African Caribbean dance. The company eventually becomes the Katherine Dunham Group.

1938 On June 22, Joe Louis beats Max Schmeling in a rematch of his 1936 defeat by the German boxer.

Jacob Lawrence holds his first solo exhibition at the Harlem YMCA and completes his *Toussaint L'Ouverture* series.

In November, Crystal Bird Fauset of Philadelphia becomes the first African American woman elected to a state legislature when she is chosen to serve in the Pennsylvania House of Representatives.

On December 12, the U.S. Supreme Court in *Missouri ex rel. Gaines v. Canada* rules that a state that provides in-state education for whites must provide comparable in-state education for blacks. The plaintiff, Lloyd Gaines, mysteriously disappears after the Court's decision.

1939 Popular contralto Marian Anderson sings at Lincoln Memorial before seventy-five thousand people on Easter Sunday after the Daughters of the American Revolution refuse to allow her to perform at Constitution Hall.

Bill "Bojangles" Robinson organizes the Black Actors Guild.

World War II begins in Europe on September 1 when Germany invades Poland.

Jane M. Bolin becomes the first African American woman judge in the United States when she is appointed to the domestic relations court of New York City.

1940 Census of 1940.
U.S. population: 131,669,275
Black population: 12,865,518 (9.8 percent)

On February 29, Hattie McDaniel receives the Best Supporting Actress Oscar for her role in *Gone With the Wind*. She becomes the first black actor to win an Academy Award.

Richard Wright publishes his first novel, *Native Son.*

Dr. Charles R. Drew presents his thesis, "Banked Blood," at Columbia-Presbyterian Medical Center in New York. The thesis includes his research, which discovers that plasma can replace whole blood transfusions.

In October, Benjamin Oliver Davis is named the first African American general in the regular army.

Booker T. Washington becomes the first African American portrayed on a U.S. postage stamp.

1941 Mary Lucinda Dawson founds the National Negro Opera Company.

The U.S. Army creates the Tuskegee Air Squadron.

The U.S. Supreme Court rules that separate facilities on railroads must be equal.

On June 25, President Franklin Roosevelt issues Executive Order 8802, which desegregates U.S. defense plans and shipyards and creates the Fair Employment Practices Committee (FEPC). The order comes after A. Philip Randolph and other civil rights leaders threaten a march of fifty thousand on Washington on July 1, 1941, to protest racial employment discrimination in the defense facilities.

On December 8, the United States enters World War II following the attack on Pearl Harbor. Dorie Miller is awarded the Navy Cross for his heroism during that battle.

1941–45 The desperate need for labor in U.S. defense plants and shipyards leads to the migration of 1.2 million African Americans from the South to the North and West. This migration transforms American politics as blacks increasingly vote in their new homes and put pressure on Congress to protect civil rights throughout the nation. Their activism lays much of the foundation for the national civil rights movement a decade later.

1942 Margaret Walker publishes *For My People*.

The Congress of Racial Equality (CORE) is founded in Chicago by James Farmer, Jr., George Houser, and Bernice Fisher.

The U.S. Marine Corps accepts African American men for the first time.

Charity Adams becomes the first black woman commissioned officer in the Women's Army Auxiliary Corps (WAACs).

1943 The Naval Academy at Annapolis and other naval officer schools accept African American men for the first time.

The Detroit Race Riot, June 20–21, claims thirty-four lives, including twenty-five African Americans. Other riots occur in Harlem; Mobile, Alabama; and Beaumont, Texas.

Protesting racial discrimination, the newly formed CORE stages its first successful sit-in at a Chicago restaurant.

Running on the Communist Party Ticket, Benjamin Davis is elected to fill the seat of Adam Clayton Powell on the New York City Council. He is the first black Communist elected to political office. He wins a full term in 1945 and serves until 1949.

The first black cadets graduate from the Army Flight School at Tuskegee Institute, Alabama.

By summer, fourteen thousand African American soldiers of the Ninety-third Infantry Division and the Thirty-second and Thirty-third companies of the Women's Army Auxiliary Corps (approximately three hundred women) are stationed in the Arizona desert at Fort Huachuca for training. They are the largest concentration of black military personnel on one base in the history of the nation.

Two US Navy destroyers, the USS *Mason* and the submarine chaser *PC1264*, are staffed entirely by African American crews.

The black Ninety-ninth Pursuit Squadron (Tuskegee Airmen) flies its first combat mission in Italy.

1944 On April 3, the U.S. Supreme Court in *Smith v. Allwright* declares white-only political primaries unconstitutional.

Frederick Douglass Patterson establishes the United Negro College Fund on April 25 to help support black colleges and black students.

Reverend Adam Clayton Powell, pastor of the Abyssinian Baptist Church in New York City, is elected to Congress from Harlem in November.

Gunnar Myrdal publishes *An American Dilemma*.

The "Golden Thirteen" become the first black commissioned officers in the U.S. Navy.

The U.S. Navy orders the crews of all naval vessels integrated.

African American military color guard
during World War II.

1945 President Franklin Delano Roosevelt dies on April 12.

The United Nations is founded at San Francisco on April 25.

On May 8, Germany surrenders on VE day.

Colonel Benjamin O. Davis, Jr., is named commander of Goodman Field, Kentucky. He is the first African American to command a military base.

Japan surrenders on VJ day, ending World War II on September 2. By the end of the war, one million African American men and women have served in the U.S. military.

Nat King Cole becomes the first African American to have a radio variety show. The show airs on NBC.

Todd Duncan becomes the first African American permanent member of the New York City Opera.

Frederick C. Branch becomes the first African American U.S. Marine Corps officer.

Ebony magazine publishes its first issue on November 1.

1946 Dr. Charles S. Johnson becomes the first African American president of Fisk University.

The U.S. Supreme Court, in *Morgan v. Virginia*, rules that segregation in interstate bus travel is unconstitutional.

1947 On April 10, Jackie Robinson of the Brooklyn Dodgers becomes the first African American to play major league baseball in the twentieth century.

The NAACP petition on racism, "An Appeal to the World," is presented to the United Nations.

Texas Southern University is established in Houston, Texas.

President Harry S. Truman's Committee on Civil Rights issues *To Secure These Rights*, the largest study of civil rights violations and proposed remedies ever advanced by the federal government.

1948 On July 26, President Harry Truman issues Executive Order 9981, directing the desegregation of the armed forces.

Alice Coachman becomes the first African American woman to win an Olympic Gold Medal. She wins the high jump competition in the London Olympics.

The United States Supreme Court, in *Shelley v. Kraemer,* rules that racially restrictive covenants are legally unenforceable.

The U.S. Supreme Court rules, in *Sipuel v. Board of Regents of the University of Oklahoma,* that the state must admit qualified African American students to its previously all-white graduate schools when no comparable black institutions are available.

On October 1, the California Supreme Court voids the law banning interracial marriages in the state.

James Baskett becomes the first black man to receive an Academy Award. He is given an Honorary Academy Award for his portrayal of "Uncle Remus" in the 1946 film, *Song of the South.*

Don Barksdale becomes the first African American to play on an Olympic basketball team. When his team wins at the London Olympics, he becomes the first black player to earn a Gold Medal in basketball.

1949 In June, Wesley Brown becomes the first African American to graduate from the Naval Academy at Annapolis.

Atlanta businessman Jesse Blanton, Sr., establishes WERD-AM, the first black-owned radio station. It begins broadcasting in the city on October 3.

1950 Census of 1950.
U.S. population: 150,697,361
Black population: 15,044,937 (10 percent)

On May 1, Gwendolyn Brooks of Chicago becomes the first African American to receive a Pulitzer Prize. She wins the prize in poetry.

On September 22, Ralph Bunche becomes the first African American recipient of a Nobel Peace Prize for his mediation of a settlement between Arabs and Israelis in the 1947–48 Mideast Crisis.

Dr. Helen O. Dickens becomes the first African American woman admitted to the American College of Surgeons.

The National Basketball Association (NBA) accepts its first three black players: Earl Lloyd (Washington Capitols), Chuck Cooper (Boston Celtics), and Nat "Sweetwater" Clifton (New York Knicks).

Ethel Waters becomes the first African American star of a network television series, *Beulah*.

The United States Supreme Court, in *Sweatt v. Painter*, rules that the states must make equal educational facilities available to African American graduate and professional students.

The U.S. Supreme Court, in *McLaurin v. Oklahoma*, outlaws classroom segregation based on race.

In *Henderson v. United States Et Al.*, the U.S. Supreme Court rules that railroad dining car segregation is unequal treatment and thus violates the Interstate Commerce Act.

1951 On May 24, the U.S. Supreme Court rules that racial segregation in District of Columbia restaurants is unconstitutional.

On May 24, a mob of thirty-five hundred whites attempt to prevent a black family from moving into a Cicero, Illinois, apartment. Illinois governor Adlai Stevenson calls out the Illinois National Guard to protect the family and restore order.

Harry T. Moore, a Florida NAACP official, is killed by a bomb in Mims, Florida, on December 25.

1952 The Tuskegee Institute reports no lynchings in the United States for the first time in seventy-one years of tabulation.

On March 30, Los Angeles newspaper owner and editor Charlotta Bass is nominated for vice president on the Progressive Party ticket at its Chicago convention in March (along with Vincent Hallinan, who is the party's presidential candidate). Bass, nominated at the convention by Paul Robeson with W. E. B. Du Bois seconding the nomination, is the first African American woman to be selected for the vice presidential slot.

Colonel Benjamin O. Davis, Jr., is appointed commander of the Fifty-first Fighter Interceptor Wing in Korea.

Ralph Ellison publishes *Invisible Man.*

Cora Brown of Detroit becomes the first black woman elected to a state senate seat (Michigan State Senate).

1953 On June 19, Baton Rouge, Louisiana, African Americans begin a boycott of their city's segregated municipal bus line.

On December 31, Hulan Jack becomes the first African American borough president of Manhattan. At the time he is the highest-ranking black municipal elected official in the nation.

1954 On May 17, the United States Supreme Court, in *Brown v. Board of Education,* declares segregation in all public schools in the United States unconstitutional, nullifying the earlier judicial doctrine of "separate but equal."

On October 27, Benjamin Oliver Davis, Jr., becomes the first black Air Force general.

Malcolm X becomes minister of the Nation of Islam's Harlem Temple 7.

Dr. Peter Murray Marshall is installed as president of the New York County (Manhattan) Medical Society. He is the first African American to lead a division of the American Medical Association.

On November 1, actress Dorothy Dandridge becomes the first black person on the cover of a major magazine when she appears on *Life* magazine.

1955 Fourteen-year-old Chicago resident Emmett Till is lynched in Money, Mississippi, on August 28.

Chuck Berry, an early breakthrough rock-and-roll artist, records "Maybellene."

Rosa Parks refuses to relinquish her bus seat to a white man on December 1, initiating the Montgomery Bus Boycott. Soon afterward, Martin Luther King, Jr., becomes the leader of the boycott.

The U.S. Supreme Court prohibits the segregation of recreational facilities, such as playgrounds.

The U.S. Supreme Court in *Brown II* reiterates the Court's 1954 Brown decision and mandates that school desegregation proceed with "all deliberate speed."

1956 Autherine Lucy is admitted to the University of Alabama on February 3. She is suspended on February 7 after a riot ensues at the university to protest her presence. Lucy is expelled on February 29.

On November 11, Nat King Cole becomes the first African American man to host a prime-time variety show on national television. He appears on NBC.

On November 13, the U.S. Supreme Court, in *Gayle v. Browder,* bans segregation in intrastate travel, effectively giving a victory to those supporting the Montgomery Bus Boycott.

1957 Congress passes the Civil Rights Act of 1957, the first legislation protecting black rights since Reconstruction. The act establishes the Civil Rights section of the Justice Department and empowers federal prosecutors to obtain court injunctions against interference with the right to vote. It also creates the federal Civil Rights Commission, with the authority to investigate discriminatory conditions and recommend corrective measures.

Dorothy Irene Height is appointed president of the National Council of Negro Women, a position she holds for forty-one years. She later launches a crusade for justice for black women and works to strengthen the black family.

On July 6, Althea Gibson becomes the first African American to win the Women's Singles Division of the British Tennis Championship at Wimbledon.

In September, President Dwight D. Eisenhower sends federal troops to Little Rock, Arkansas, to ensure the enforcement of a federal court order to desegregate Central High School and to protect nine African American students enrolled as part of the order. The troops remain at the high school until the end of the school year.

1958 On January 12, the Southern Christian Leadership Conference (SCLC) is organized in Atlanta with Dr. Martin Luther King, Jr., as its first president.

The Alvin Ailey Dance Theater is formed in New York.

Louis E. Lomax becomes the first African American newscaster. He works for WNTA-TV in New York City.

Ruth Carol Taylor becomes the first African American flight attendant when she is hired by Mohawk Airlines of New York.

1959 On January 12, Berry Gordy, Jr., founds Motown Records in Detroit.

Lorraine Hansberry's *A Raisin in the Sun* opens on March 11 with Sidney Poitier in the starring role. It is the first play by an African American woman to be produced on Broadway.

On April 26, Mack Charles Parker is lynched near Poplarville, Mississippi.

Ella Fitzgerald and Count Basie receive two awards each at the first Grammy Awards Ceremony.

1960 Census of 1960.
U.S. population: 179,323,175
Black population: 18,871,831 (10.6 percent)

On February 1, four students from North Carolina Agricultural and Technical College in Greensboro

begin a sit-in at Woolworth's Drug Store to protest company policy that bans African Americans
from sitting at its counters.

On April 15, 150 black and white students from
across the South gather at Shaw University in
Raleigh, North Carolina, to form the Student
Nonviolent Coordinating Committee (SNCC).

The Civil Rights Act of 1960 is signed into law by
President Dwight D. Eisenhower on May 6. The
act establishes federal inspection of local voter
registration rolls and introduces penalties for
anyone who obstructs a citizen's attempt to
register to vote or to cast a ballot.

Track star Wilma Rudolph of Tennessee State
University is the first woman to win three Gold
Medals at the Olympic Games, held that year
in Rome.

On November 8, Massachusetts senator John F.
Kennedy defeats Vice President Richard Nixon
in one of the closest elections in history. Many
observers credit African American voters with
Kennedy's narrow margin of victory.

1961 The Congress of Racial Equality organizes Freedom Rides through the Deep South.

Riots on the University of Georgia campus in
September fail to prevent the enrollment of

the institution's first two African American students, Hamilton Holmes and Charlayne Hunter (Gault).

The DuSable Museum of African American History is founded in Chicago by Margaret and Charles Burroughs. It is the first of the major African American community museums.

1962 Ernie Davis, a running back at Syracuse University, becomes the first African American athlete to win college football's Heisman Trophy.

On October 1, James Meredith becomes the first black student to enroll at the University of Mississippi. On the day he enters the university, he is escorted by U.S. marshals after federal troops are sent in to suppress rioting and maintain order.

1963 Martin Luther King, Jr., writes his "Letter from Birmingham Jail" on April 16.

On May 3, Birmingham police use dogs and fire hoses to attack civil rights demonstrators.

Despite Governor George Wallace's vow to "block the schoolhouse door" to prevent their enrollment on June 11, Vivian Malone and James Hood register for classes at the University of Alabama. They are the first African American students to attend the university.

James Baldwin publishes *The Fire Next Time.*

On June 12, Mississippi NAACP field secretary Medgar Evers is assassinated outside his home in Jackson.

Over two hundred thousand people gather in Washington, D.C., on August 28 as part of the March on Washington, an unprece-dented demonstration demanding civil rights and equal opportunity for African Americans. Martin Luther King, Jr., delivers his "I have a dream" speech here.

On September 15, the Sixteenth Street Baptist Church is bombed in Birmingham, Alabama, killing four girls, Addie Mae Collins, Denise McNair, Carole Robertson, and Cynthia Wesley, ages eleven to fourteen.

President John F. Kennedy is assassinated in Dallas on November 22.

Martin Luther King, Jr., is named *Time* magazine's Man of the Year.

1964 On January 8, President Lyndon Johnson, in his first State of the Union Address, "declares uncon-ditional war on poverty in America," thus initiating a broad array of government programs designed to assist the poorest citizens of the nation, including a disproportionate number of African Americans.

Sidney Poitier wins an Academy Award for Best Actor for his performance in the film *Lilies of the Field.*

SNCC organizes the Mississippi Freedom Summer Project.

On February 25, Cassius Clay (later Muhammad Ali) wins the first of three World Heavyweight Championships in a bout with Sonny Liston in Miami, Florida.

On March 12, Malcolm X announces his break with the Nation of Islam and his founding of the Muslim Mosque in Harlem.

On June 21, civil rights workers James Chaney, Andrew Goodman, and Michael Schwerner are abducted and killed by terrorists in Mississippi.

The Civil Rights Act of 1964 is passed by Congress on July 2. The act bans discrimination in all public accommodations and by employers. It also establishes the Equal Opportunity Employment Commission (EEOC) to monitor compliance with the law.

The Mississippi Freedom Democratic Party (MFDP) delegation, led by Fannie Lou Hamer, is denied seating at the Democratic National Convention in Atlantic City in August.

On August 20, President Lyndon Johnson signs the Economic Opportunity Act, initiating the federally sponsored War on Poverty. The act includes Head Start, Upward Bound, and Volunteers in Service to America (VISTA).

The Twenty-fourth Amendment to the Constitution, which abolishes the poll tax, is ratified.

On December 10, Martin Luther King, Jr., receives the Nobel Peace Prize in Stockholm, Sweden.

1965 Malcolm X is assassinated at the Audubon Ballroom in Harlem on February 21.

On March 7, six hundred Alabama civil rights activists stage a Selma-to-Montgomery protest march to draw attention to the continued denial of black voting rights in the state. The marchers are confronted by Alabama state troopers, whose attack on them at the Edmund Pettus Bridge is carried on national television. On March 21, Martin Luther King, Jr., leads a five-day, fifty-four-mile march retracing the route of the original activists. The thirty-three hundred marchers at the beginning of the trek eventually grow to twenty-five thousand when they reach the Alabama capitol on March 25. After the protest march, President Lyndon Johnson proposes the Voting Rights Act to guarantee black voting throughout the South.

A 1965 New York City civil rights march.

In March, the White House releases "The Negro Family: The Case for National Action," popularly known as the Moynihan Report.

On June 4, President Lyndon Johnson first uses the term "affirmative action" in a speech at Howard University.

Alex Haley publishes the *Autobiography of Malcolm X*.

The Voting Rights Act is signed into law by President Lyndon Johnson on August 6.

The Watts Uprising occurs on August 11–16. Thirty-four people are killed and one thousand are injured in the five-day confrontation.

Maulana Ron Karenga founds the black nationalist organization US in Los Angeles following the Watts Uprising.

Bill Cosby costars with Robert Culp in the television series *I Spy*. With the premier episode, Cosby becomes the first African American to costar in a network drama.

Patricia Roberts Harris becomes the first black woman envoy when she is appointed U.S. ambassador to Luxembourg.

1966 When Robert O. Lowery is appointed the fire commissioner for New York City on January 1 by New York City mayor John V. Lindsay, he becomes the first African American to head a major city fire department.

On January 13, Robert Weaver, President Lyndon Johnson's nominee to head the newly created Department of Housing and Urban Development, is confirmed for the post by the U.S. Senate. Weaver becomes the first African American to hold a cabinet post.

On January 25, Constance Baker Motley is appointed by President Lyndon Johnson to the federal bench in New York City. She becomes the first African American woman elevated to a federal judgeship.

When Bill Russell assumes the head coaching post for the Boston Celtics in the summer, he becomes the first African American head coach in the history of the National Basketball Association (NBA).

In May, Stokely Carmichael becomes chairman of SNCC and embraces the concept of "black power."

On June 5, James Meredith begins a solitary March Against Fear for 220 miles from Memphis, Tennessee, to Jackson, Mississippi, to protest racial discrimination. Meredith is shot by a sniper soon after crossing into Mississippi. Civil rights leaders, including Martin Luther King, Jr. (SCLC), Floyd McKissick (CORE), and Stokely Carmichael (SNCC), vow to continue the march, which eventually reaches Jackson. While in Greenwood, Carmichael gives his first "black power" speech, on June 26.

On October 15, the Black Panther Party is formed in Oakland, California, by Bobby Seale and Huey P. Newton.

Andrew F. Brimmer is appointed by President Lyndon Johnson to be the first African American to serve on the Federal Reserve Board.

James T. Whitehead, Jr., becomes the first African American to pilot a U-2 spy plane.

On November 8, Edward Brooke of Massachusetts becomes the first African American to be elected to the U.S. Senate since Reconstruction.

On November 8, Julian Bond wins a seat in the Georgia State Senate. However, he is denied the seat by the Georgia Legislature because of his opposition to the Vietnam War. Bond is eventually seated after a bitter court battle.

1967 On April 4, Martin Luther King, Jr., delivers "Beyond Vietnam: A Time to Break Silence" at a meeting of Clergy and Laity Concerned at Riverside Church in New York City.

H. Rap Brown becomes chairman of SNCC on May 12.

On June 12, the U.S. Supreme Court, in *Loving v. Virginia,* strikes down state interracial marriage bans.

The six-day Newark Riot begins on July 12. In total: 23 die, 725 are injured, and 1,500 are arrested.

Thurgood Marshall takes his seat as the first African American Justice on the U.S. Supreme Court on July 13.

On July 23, Detroit erupts. Between July 23 and July 28, 43 are killed, 1,189 are injured, and over 7,000 are arrested.

On November 13, Carl Stokes and Richard G. Hatcher are elected the first black mayors of Cleveland, Ohio; and Gary, Indiana, respectively.

1968 On February 8, three students at South Carolina State College in Orangeburg are killed by police in what will be known as the Orangeburg Massacre.

On February 29, the Report of the National Advisory Commission on Civil Disorders, popularly known as the Kerner Report, is released. The report analyzes the 1967 race riots and concludes ominously, "Our nation is moving toward two societies, one black, one white—separate and unequal."

Martin Luther King, Jr., is assassinated in Memphis, Tennessee, on April 4. In the wake of the assassination, 125 cities in twenty-nine states experience uprisings. By April 11, forty-six people are killed and thirty-five thousand are injured in these confrontations.

In April, Congress enacts the Civil Rights Act of 1968, which outlaws discrimination in the sale and rental of housing.

New York senator and presidential candidate Robert F. Kennedy is assassinated on June 5 in Los Angeles.

On June 19, the Poor People's Campaign brings fifty thousand demonstrators to Washington, D.C.

Arthur Ashe becomes the first African American to win the Men's Singles competition in the U.S. Open.

In September, Marlin Oliver Briscoe becomes the first African American quarterback in modern National Football League history when he joins the Denver Broncos in his rookie season.

San Francisco State University establishes the nation's first black studies program in September.

The Studio Museum in Harlem opens as the first fine arts museum devoted exclusively to African American works.

In November, Shirley Chisholm of New York becomes the first black woman elected to the U.S. Congress.

1969 The Ford Foundation gives $1 million to Morgan State University, Howard University, and Yale University to help prepare faculty members to teach courses in African American studies.

On May 5, Moneta Sleet, Jr., of *Ebony* magazine becomes the first African American to win a Pulitzer Prize in Photography.

On September 22, the African American studies program begins offering courses at Harvard University.

Alfred Day Hershey, Ph.D., a geneticist, becomes the first African American to share a Nobel Prize in Medicine when he is recognized for his work on the replication and genetic structure of viruses.

Robert Chrisman and Nathan Hare publish the first issue of *The Black Scholar* in November.

Howard N. Lee becomes the first African American mayor of Chapel Hill, North Carolina. At the time he is the first African American mayor of a predominantly white Southern city.

On December 4, Chicago police kill Black Panther leaders Fred Hampton and Mark Clarke.

1970 Census of 1970.
U.S. population: 204,765,770
Black population: 22,580,289 (11.1 percent)

Dr. Clifton Wharton, Jr., is named president of Michigan State University on January 2. He is the first African American to lead a major, predominantly white university in the twentieth century.

On February 18, Bobby Seale and six other defendants (popularly known as the Chicago Seven) are acquitted of the charge of conspiring to disrupt the 1968 Democratic National Convention.

The first issue of *Essence* magazine appears in May.

On May 15, two students, Philip Lafayette Gibbs and James Earl Green, are killed by police in a confrontation with students at Jackson State University in Jackson, Mississippi.

On July 1, Kenneth Gibson becomes the first black mayor of an eastern city when he assumes the post in Newark, New Jersey.

The first issue of *Black Enterprise* magazine appears in August.

The San Rafael, California, courthouse shooting on August 7 results in the death of Judge Harold Haley and three others, including Jonathan Jackson, the younger brother of imprisoned Black

Panther George Jackson. UCLA philosophy professor Angela Davis is implicated in the shooting and becomes the subject of a nationwide FBI-led search. Davis is captured and brought to trial. She is acquitted of all charges on June 4, 1972.

On October 12, Charles Gordone becomes the first African American to win a Pulitzer Prize in Drama in his play *No Place to Be Somebody*.

The Joint Center for Political Studies is established in Washington, D.C.

LeRoy Henderson

Political activist Angela Davis.

1971 On January 12, the Congressional Black Caucus is formed in Washington, D.C.

In July, Captain Samuel L. Gravely, Jr., is promoted to rear admiral. He becomes the first African American to achieve flag rank in the U.S. Navy.

On September 9, nearly twelve hundred inmates seize control of half of the New York State Prison at Attica. Four days later twenty-nine inmates and ten hostages are killed when state troopers and correctional officers suppress the uprising.

The U.S. Supreme Court rules, in *Griggs v. Duke Power Company,* that the utility corporation's standardized aptitude testing of its workers for promotion is part of the company's long-standing policy of using such requirements to give job preferences to its white employees.

On December 18, Reverend Jesse Jackson founds People United to Save Humanity (PUSH) in Chicago.

1972 On March 10–12, more than three thousand delegates and five thousand observers gather in Gary, Indiana, for the first National Black Political Convention. The convention issues the Gary Declaration.

Over the summer, New York congresswoman Shirley Chisholm makes an unsuccessful bid for the Democratic presidential nomination. She is the first African American to campaign for the nomination.

In November, Barbara Jordan of Houston and Andrew Young of Atlanta become the first black congressional representatives elected from the U.S. South since 1898.

The first Haitian "boat people" arrive in south Florida.

U.S. Representative Shirley Chisholm.

LeRoy Henderson

1973 On May 29, Thomas Bradley is elected the first black mayor of Los Angeles in the modern era. He is reelected four times and thus holds the mayor's office for twenty years.

The National Black Feminist Organization is established.

Marion Wright Edelman creates the Children's Defense Fund.

The U.S. Supreme Court in *Keyes v. School District No. 1, Denver, Colorado,* issues its first major ruling in a school segregation case outside the South. The court orders the Denver School District to craft a desegregation plan.

On October 16, Maynard H. Jackson, Jr., is elected the first black mayor of Atlanta.

On November 6, Coleman Young is elected the first black mayor of Detroit.

1974 On April 8, Henry "Hank" Aaron hits his 715th home run to become the all-time leader in home runs in major league baseball.

On June 21, U.S. District Judge W. Arthur Garrity, in the *Morgan v. Hennigan* ruling, initiates a busing program involving several thousand students, designed to desegregate the public schools of Boston.

The largest single gift to date from a black organization is $132,000, given by the Links, Inc., to the United Negro College Fund on July 1.

On October 30, Muhammad Ali defeats George Foreman in Kinshasa, Zaire, to regain the World Heavyweight Championship.

On November 5, George Brown and Mervyn Dymally are elected lieutenant governors of Colorado and California, respectively. They are the first African Americans to hold these posts in the twentieth century.

1975 The Morehouse School of Medicine (Atlanta) becomes the only black medical school established in the United States in the twentieth century. The first dean and president of Morehouse School of Medicine is Dr. Louis Sullivan, who later becomes the U.S. surgeon general.

Wallace D. Muhammad assumes control of the Nation of Islam after the death of his father, Elijah Muhammad. He changes the organization's direction and its name to the World Community of al-Islam.

Arthur Ashe becomes the first African American to win the British Men's Singles at Wimbledon.

General Daniel "Chappie" James of the Air Force becomes the first African American four-star general.

The first black-owned television station, WGPR, begins broadcasting in Detroit.

On October 12, Frank Robinson becomes the first black major league baseball manager when he takes over the Cleveland Indians.

Time magazine for the first time names two black women, Congresswoman Barbara Jordan and labor activist Addie L. Wyatt, vice president of the Amalgamated Meat Cutters Union, as Persons of the Year.

Of mixed heritage, Pittsburgh fullback Franco Harris becomes the first African American and the first Italian American to win the Super Bowl Most Valuable Player Award in the National Football League.

1976 The United States Naval Academy at Annapolis admits women for the first time in June. Janie L. Mines becomes the first African American woman cadet to enter. She graduates in 1980.

College and university enrollment for African American students rises sharply, from 282,000 in 1966 to 1,062,000 in 1976.

Vice Admiral Samuel Lee Gravely is appointed commander of the Third Fleet. He will oversee operations on one hundred navy warships and command over sixty thousand sailors and marines.

1977 In January, Patricia Harris is appointed by President Jimmy Carter to head the U.S. Department of Housing and Urban Development. She becomes the first African American woman to hold a cabinet position.

In January, Congressman Andrew Young is appointed by President Jimmy Carter to be U.S. ambassador to the United Nations. He is the first African American to hold that post.

The eighth and final night for the televised miniseries based on Alex Haley's *Roots* is shown on February 3. This final episode achieves the highest ratings to that point for a single television program.

On March 8, Henry L. Marsh, III, becomes the first African American mayor of Richmond, Virginia.

In September, Randall Robinson founds TransAfrica, a lobbying group for Africa, in Washington, D.C.

1978 Minister Louis Farrakhan breaks with the World Community of al-Islam and becomes the leader of the revived Nation of Islam.

On June 28, the U.S. Supreme Court in *Regents of the University of California v. Bakke* narrowly upholds affirmative action as a legal strategy for addressing past discrimination.

On September 15, Muhammad Ali becomes the first boxer to win the World Heavyweight Championship three times when he defeats Leon Spinks at the Superdome in New Orleans.

In September, Max Robinson becomes the first African American coanchor of an evening news broadcast, ABC's *World News Tonight*. Robinson remains with ABC in that capacity until 1983, when cohost Peter Jennings becomes the sole anchor.

Dr. LaSalle D. Leffall becomes the first African American president of the American Cancer Society.

1979 The Sugarhill Gang records "Rapper's Delight" in Harlem.

Franklin Thomas is named president of the Ford Foundation. He is the first African American to head a major philanthropic foundation.

Frank E. Petersen, Jr., becomes the first African American to earn the rank of general in the U.S. Marines.

In September, Hazel W. Johnson becomes the first African American woman to be promoted to the rank of general in the U.S. Army.

The U.S. Supreme Court, in *United Steelworkers of America, AFL-CIO v. Weber,* rules that training schemes specifically crafted to assist minorities are legitimate because such programs are consistent with the 1964 Civil Rights Act, which seeks to eliminate patterns of segregation and discrimination.

Richard Arrington, Jr., is elected the first African American mayor of Birmingham, Alabama.

The Nobel Prize in Economics goes to Sir Arthur Lewis of Princeton University. He is the first black person to win the award in a category other than peace.

1980 Census of 1980.
U.S. population: 226,504,825
Black population: 26,482,349 (11.8 percent)

In January, Willie Lewis Brown, Jr., becomes the first African American speaker in a state legislature when he is selected for the post in the California Assembly. Brown holds the speakership until 1995, when he is elected mayor of San Francisco.

On May 17–18, rioting breaks out in Liberty City, Florida (near Miami), after police officers are acquitted for killing an unarmed black man. The riot, which generates fifteen deaths, is the worst in the nation since Detroit in 1967.

Toni Cade Bambara's *The Salt Eaters* wins the American Book Award.

Robert L. Johnson begins operation of Black Entertainment Television (BET) out of Washington, D.C.

Dr. Levi Watkins, Jr., becomes the first physician to place an automatic defibrillator in a human heart to regulate blood flow.

The U.S. Supreme Court, in *Fullilove v. Klutznick,* holds that the creation of minority set-aside programs are a legitimate exercise of congressional power.

1981 Pamela McAllister Johnson becomes the first African American woman to publish a widely circulated newspaper, the *Ithaca Journal* (New York).

On October 18, the Martin Luther King, Jr., Library and Archives opens in Atlanta, Georgia.

On December 20, the musical *Dreamgirls* opens on Broadway with Jennifer Holliday, who eventually wins a Tony for her performance as Effie.

1982 The struggle of Reverend Ben Chavis and his followers to block a toxic waste dump in Warren County, North Carolina, launches a national campaign against environmental racism.

Bryant Gumbel is named anchor of *The Today Show,* becoming the first African American to hold the post on a major network.

Clarence Thomas is nominated by President Ronald Reagan to become the chair of the Equal Employment Opportunity Commission (EEOC). His nomination is confirmed by the U.S. Senate.

On June 30, President Ronald Reagan extends the Voting Rights Act of 1965.

Alice Walker's book *The Color Purple* is released. The book eventually wins the American Book Award and the Pulitzer Prize in Literature in 1983. It also becomes the basis for the film of the same name, directed by Steven Spielberg.

Charles Fuller wins the Pulitzer Prize in Drama for his play *A Soldier's Story,* which is the basis for the 1984 film of the same title.

Clifton E. Wharton, Jr., becomes the first African American elected as chairman of the Rockefeller Foundation.

1983 On April 12, Harold Washington is elected the first black mayor of Chicago.

On August 30, Guion (Guy) S. Bluford, Jr., a crew member on the *Challenger,* becomes the first African American astronaut to make a space flight.

On September 18, Vanessa Williams becomes the first African American crowned Miss America in Atlantic City. In July 1984, she relinquishes her crown when nude photos of her appear in *Penthouse* magazine.

Harvey Bernard Gantt becomes the first African American mayor of Charlotte, North Carolina.

At the end of 1983, African Americans are mayors in a number of major cities including Chicago, Charlotte, Los Angeles, Detroit, New Orleans, Atlanta, Birmingham, and Washington, D.C.

On November 2, President Ronald Reagan signs into law a bill making the third Monday in January a federal holiday honoring the life of Martin Luther King, Jr.

Michael Jackson releases the album *Thriller,* which wins eight Grammy Awards and becomes the biggest-selling record in U.S. history, with over thirty million copies sold around the world.

1984 On January 2, W. Wilson Goode becomes the first African American mayor of Philadelphia.

On January 5, New York City mayor Edward I. Koch names Benjamin Ward the first African American police commissioner of New York City.

In January, Reverend Jesse Jackson travels to Syria to negotiate the release of U.S. Air Force pilot Robert Goodman, who had been shot down over that country. Jackson returns to the United States with the freed pilot.

Reverend Jesse Jackson wins approximately one-fourth of the votes cast in the Democratic primaries and caucuses and about one-eighth of the convention delegates in a losing bid for the Democratic presidential nomination.

In August, Carl Lewis wins four Gold Medals at the Olympics in Los Angeles, matching the record set by Jesse Owens in 1936.

In September, *The Cosby Show* makes its television debut. The show runs for eight seasons and becomes the most successful series in television history, featuring a mostly African American cast.

Former Philadelphia congressman Robert C. Nix becomes the first African American chief justice of the Pennsylvania Supreme Court.

Russell Simmons forms Def Jam Records in Harlem.

Rev. Jesse Jackson.

1985 In May, Philadelphia's African American mayor, Wilson Goode, orders the Philadelphia police to bomb the headquarters of MOVE, a local black nationalist organization. The bombing leaves 11 people dead and 250 homeless.

U.S. Representative William H. Gray III (Pennsylvania), becomes the first African American congressman to chair the House Budget Committee.

Sherian Grace Cadoria is promoted to brigadier general of the U.S. Army. She becomes the highest-ranking woman of color in the armed forces.

Congressman John Conyers (Michigan) introduces the Anti-Apartheid Act, which would impose economic sanctions on South Africa for its refusal to grant civil rights to the majority of its citizens.

The U.S. Supreme Court, in *Wygant Et Al. v. Jackson Board of Education Et Al.*, rules that a collective bargaining agreement between the Jackson (Mississippi) Board of Education and a teacher's union that permits nonminority teachers to be laid off before minority teachers with less seniority is a violation of the Equal Protection Clause of the Fourteenth Amendment to the Constitution.

Air Force captain Donnie Cochran becomes the first black member of the U.S. Navy's Blue Angels Flight Demonstration Squadron. Nine years later (1994) Cochran commands the Blue Angels.

1986 On January 20, the first national Martin Luther King, Jr., holiday is celebrated.

On January 28, Dr. Ronald McNair and six other crew members die when the space shuttle *Challenger* explodes shortly after launch from the Kennedy Space Center in Florida.

Mike Tyson wins the World Boxing Council's Heavyweight Championship title. At twenty he is the youngest boxer to ever hold the title.

Spike Lee releases his first feature film, *She's Gotta Have It,* initiating a new wave of interest in black films and African American filmmakers.

On September 8, *The Oprah Winfrey Show* from Chicago becomes nationally syndicated.

In November, Mike Espy becomes only the second African American (and the first in the twentieth century) to win a congressional seat in Mississippi.

Willy T. Ribbs becomes the first black Formula One race car driver. Five years later he becomes the first black driver to qualify for the Indianapolis 500 auto race.

1987 Rita Dove wins the Pulitzer Prize in Poetry.

Toni Morrison wins the Pulitzer Prize in Literature.

On August 6, Reginald Lewis orchestrates the leveraged buyout of Beatrice Foods to become the first African American CEO of a billion-dollar corporation.

Neurosurgeon Dr. Ben Carson makes medical history when he leads a seventy-member surgical team at Johns Hopkins Hospital in a twenty-two-hour operation separating Siamese twins (the Binder twins), who are joined at the cranium.

On October 28, Brigadier General Fred A. Gordon is appointed commandant of the cadets at the U.S. Military Academy at West Point.

Clifton R. Wharton, Jr., is appointed chairman and CEO of TIAA-CREF, the nineteenth-largest U.S. Fortune 500 company. He becomes the first black chairman and CEO of a major U.S. corporation.

On December 8, Kurt Lidell Schmoke becomes the first African American elected mayor of Baltimore.

1988 Douglas Lee (Doug) Williams is the first African American quarterback to lead his team, the Washington Redskins, to a Super Bowl victory. They defeat the Denver Broncos. Williams is named the Most Valuable Player.

Debi Thomas wins a Bronze Medal for figure skating in the Winter Olympic Games in Calgary, Canada, on February 27, 1988. She becomes the first African American to win a medal in the Winter Olympic Games.

Florence "Flo Jo" Griffith Joyner wins three Gold Medals at the 1988 Olympics in Seoul, South Korea. She dies ten years later, in 1998, of a heart seizure at the age of thirty-eight.

In his second try for the Democratic presidential nomination, Jesse L. Jackson receives 1,218 delegate votes at the Democratic National Convention on July 20. The number needed for the nomination, which goes to Michael Dukakis, is 2,082.

On November 4, comedian Bill Cosby announces his gift of $20 million to Spelman College. This is the largest donation ever made by a black American to a college or university.

Juanita Kidd Stout of Pennsylvania becomes the first African American woman elected to a state supreme court.

1989 On January 29, Barbara Harris is elected the first woman bishop of the Episcopal Church.

Philadelphia congressman William Gray III becomes the House Majority Whip. He is the first black congressman to hold that post.

On February 7, Ronald H. Brown is elected chair of the Democratic National Committee, becoming the first African American to head one of the two major political parties.

In March, Frederick Drew Gregory becomes the first African American to command a space shuttle when he leads the crew of the *Discovery.*

Houston, Texas, congressman George Thomas "Mickey" Leland is killed in a plane crash near Gambela, Ethiopia, on August 7.

Temple University in Philadelphia becomes the first American university to offer a Ph.D. degree in African American studies.

On August 10, General Colin L. Powell is named chair of the U.S. Joint Chiefs of Staff, the first African American and the youngest person (fifty-two) to hold the post.

On November 7, L. Douglas Wilder wins the governorship of Virginia, making him the first

African American to be popularly elected to that office. On the same day, David Dinkins and Norm Rice are the first African Americans elected as mayors of New York and Seattle, respectively. Notably, Dinkins defeated New York district attorney Rudolph Giuliani.

Dr. Louis W. Sullivan, president of the Morehouse College of Medicine, is nominated by President George H. W. Bush to serve as Secretary of Health and Human Services.

1990 Census of 1990.
U.S. population: 248,709,878
Black population: 29,986,060 (12 percent)

On February 11, Nelson Mandela, South African black nationalist, is freed after twenty-seven years in prison.

August Wilson wins a Pulitzer Prize in Drama for the play *The Piano Lesson*.

In November, Sharon Pratt Kelly is elected mayor of Washington, D.C. She becomes the first African American woman to lead a large American city.
Carole Ann-Marie Gist, Miss Michigan, becomes the first African American Miss USA.

Kimzy O'Neal becomes the first black "Miss Ole Miss."

188 America I AM BLACK FACTS

1991 On January 15, Roland Burris becomes the first black attorney general of Illinois.

On March 3, Los Angeles police use force to arrest Rodney King after a San Fernando Valley traffic stop. The beating of King is captured on videotape and broadcast widely, prompting an investigation and subsequent trial of three officers.

On April 10, Emanuel Cleaver II is sworn in as the first African American mayor of Kansas City, Missouri.

On June 18, Wellington Webb becomes the first African American mayor of Denver, Colorado.

On October 23, federal judge Clarence Thomas, nominated by President George H. W. Bush, is confirmed by the U.S. Senate and takes his seat on the U.S. Supreme Court. Weeks earlier Anita Hill, an African American law professor and former employee of Thomas, accuses him of sexual harassment, sparking a national debate.

Julie Dash releases *Daughters of the Dust,* the first feature film by an African American woman.

Dr. Vivian Pinn is the first woman and the first African American director of the Office of Research on Women's Health at the National Institutes of Health.

1992 In March, Willie W. Herenton is elected the first African American mayor of Memphis, Tennessee.

On April 29, a Simi Valley, California, jury acquits the three officers accused of beating Rodney King. The verdict triggers a three-day uprising in Los Angeles that results in over fifty people killed, over two thousand injured, and eight thousand arrested.

On September 12, Dr. Mae Carol Jemison becomes the first African American woman in space when she travels aboard the space shuttle *Endeavor.*

On November 3, Carol Moseley Braun of Illinois becomes the first African American woman elected to the U.S. Senate.

1993 In April, Freeman Robertson Bosley, Jr., becomes the first African American mayor of St. Louis, Missouri.

M. Joycelyn Elders becomes the first African American and the first woman to be named U.S. surgeon general on September 7.

On October 7, Toni Morrison becomes the first black American to win the Nobel Prize in Literature. The work honored is her novel *Beloved*.

Hazel R. O'Leary is appointed Secretary of the U.S. Department of Energy by President Bill Clinton.

Dr. Edward S. Cooper is the first African American elected as president of the American Heart Association.

Dr. Barbara Ross-Lee is the first African American woman to be appointed dean of a U.S. medical school, the Ohio University College of Osteopathic Medicine.

The United States Supreme Court, in *Shaw v. Reno,* rules against a North Carolina redistricting plan that creates black majority congressional districts.

1994 On June 12, O.J. Simpson's former wife, Nicole Brown Simpson, and her friend Ronald Goldman are found stabbed to death. O.J. Simpson emerges as the leading suspect and is subsequently arrested on June 17 after a two-hour low-speed pursuit of Simpson and his friend Al Cowlings that is seen on television by an estimated ninety-five million people.

1995 On October 3, after an eight-month televised trial, O.J. Simpson is acquitted of the charges of murder in the deaths of Nicole Brown Simpson and Ronald Goldman.

On May 6, Ron Kirk wins the mayoral race in Dallas, becoming the first African American mayor of the city.

The Million Man March organized by Minister Louis Farrakhan is held in Washington, D.C., on October 17.

Dr. Helene Doris Gayle becomes the first woman and the first African American director of the National Center for HIV, STD, and TB Prevention for the U.S. Centers for Disease Control.

1996 U.S. Commerce Secretary Ron Brown is killed in a plane crash near Dubrovnik, Croatia, on April 3.

On April 9, George Walker becomes the first African American to win a Pulitzer Prize in Music. The winning composition, "Lilies for Soprano or Tenor and Orchestra," is based on a poem by Walt Whitman.

In May, President Bill Clinton signs into law the Personal Responsibility and Work Opportunity Reconciliation Act, which replaces Aid to

Families with Dependent Children (AFDC) with state block grants. It also substantially cuts programs designed to help the poor.

On November 5, California voters pass Proposition 209, which outlaws affirmative action throughout the state.

In November, Dr. Donna Christian-Christensen (U.S. Virgin Islands) becomes the first woman physician and the first African American physician elected to the U.S. Congress.

J. Paul Reason becomes the first African American four-star admiral in the U.S. Navy. In *Hopwood v. State of Texas,* the U.S. Fifth Circuit Court of Appeals rules that the University of Texas cannot use race as a means of determining who is admitted to the institution.

1997 On April 13, golfer Tiger Woods wins the Master's Tournament in Augusta, Georgia. At twenty-one, he is the youngest golfer ever to win the title. He is also the first African American (or Asian American) to hold the title.

In June, Harvey Johnson, Jr., is sworn in as the first black mayor of Jackson, Mississippi.

On October 25, African American women participate in the Million Woman March in

Philadelphia, focusing on health care, education, and self-help.

In December, Lee Patrick Brown becomes Houston's first African American mayor.

1998 On June 7, James Byrd, Jr., of Jasper, Texas, accepts a ride from three white men. Two of the men, white supremacists John King and Lawrence Russell Brewer, chain Byrd to the back of a pickup truck and drag him to his death. King and Brewer are sentenced to death for the murder of Byrd while Shawn Allen Berry, the driver of the truck, is given life in prison.

Dr. David Satcher is sworn in as both the Assistant Secretary of Health and U.S. Surgeon General.

Venus Williams wins the World Tennis Association Singles, her first major title. She goes on to win the Wimbledon Women's Singles Title in 2000 and 2001.

Lillian Fishburne is the first African American woman to hold the rank of rear admiral in the U.S. Navy.

1999 On January 13, after thirteen seasons and six NBA championships, professional basketball star Michael Jordan retires from the game as a player.

On September 10, Serena Williams wins the U.S. Open Women's Singles Tennis Championship. She also wins the World Tennis Association Singles title.

Jamaican-born New Yorker Maurice Ashley is the first African American to be awarded the International Grandmaster title in chess.

Using W. E. B. Du Bois's *Encyclopedia Africana,* first proposed in 1909, as a model and inspiration, Harvard professors Henry Louis Gates and Anthony Appiah publish *Encarta Africana.*

2000 Census of 2000.
U.S. population: 281,421,906
Black population: 34,658,190 (12.3 percent)

Reverend Vashti M. McKenzie becomes the first woman bishop of the African Methodist Methodist Episcopal Church.

The 44th President of the United States,
Barack Obama.

CHAPTER SIX

INTO THE TWENTY-FIRST CENTURY

Timeline: 2001–

African American history in this new century has been dominated by important developments that reflected the elevation of black political figures to unprecedented positions in American politics. In 2001, former four-star general Colin Powell, the first African American to head the Joint Chiefs of Staff, the highest military position in the U.S. government, was selected by President George Bush to become the first African American to hold the post of secretary of state. When Powell resigned in 2005, President Bush appointed National Security Advisor Condoleezza Rice to be his successor. Rice became the first black woman and only the second woman, after Madeleine K. Albright, to hold this post.

The rise of these appointed figures, however, was eclipsed by the mercurial ascent of Barack Obama. As late as 2004,

Obama, who was first elected to the Illinois State Senate in 1994, was a relative unknown on the national political scene. In July of that year, while still campaigning for the office of U.S. senator from Illinois, Obama gave a speech before the Democratic National Convention in Boston that catapulted him into the national spotlight. Four years later Obama made political history, first by winning the nomination from front-runner Hillary Clinton, the senator from New York and wife of former president Bill Clinton. Then, on August 28, 2008, Obama officially accepted the Democratic nomination for the presidency, becoming the first African American to campaign, with his party's endorsement and support, for, and ultimately win, the highest office in the land.

The other major event of this still unfolding century was the tragedy of Hurricane Katrina in New Orleans in 2005. The storm broke the city's levees, flooding the city of nearly five hundred thousand people. Over seventeen hundred lives were lost in one of the worst disasters in U.S. history. The majority of the dead were African Americans. Despite promises of aid from federal, state, and local agencies as well as private organizations, the people of New Orleans continue to live with the consequences of the storm and its aftermath.

Other developments in this young century merit our attention even if they cannot be neatly categorized by date. First, in January 2003, U.S Census officials announced that Latinos had surpassed African Americans in population for the first time in the nation's history. Demographers agree that during this century, and perhaps as early as 2040, the United States for the first time will no longer have a European-American majority. The continued, rapid growth of the populations of Latinos, African Americans, Asian Americans, and Native Americans, and the rapidly growing biracial and multiracial populations will create a multiethnic, multiracial nation in population. The political, social, and cultural consequences of these related changes can only be imagined. Nonetheless, the United States will never again be the same for all of its peoples.

The dawn of the twenty-first century also illustrated the persistence of the consequences of centuries-old racially discriminatory policies and practices in two different but related areas: the continuing educational gap between African Americans and white and Asian America, and the growth of the prison-industrial complex with a disproportionate number of African American men and women as inmates. On May 17, 2004, on the fiftieth anniversary of the landmark *Brown v. Board of Education* ruling by the U.S. Supreme Court, black America saw a growing gap in both educational attainment and the acquisition of knowledge by many impoverished inner-city African Americans, even as the number of black college graduates stood at an all-time high. The problems in education were transformed into rising dropout rates for African American youth and other attendant developments, including persistent poverty, unemployment and underemployment, gang and other antisocial activity, teenage pregnancy, and, far too often, criminal activity. At the moment when nearly 80 percent of African Americans had escaped poverty and moved into the ranks of the middle class, approximately eight million black folks continue to live lives determined by poverty, despair, and desperation.

These developments illustrate the continuing paradox of African American history, the simultaneous dismantling of formal American apartheid, and the stubborn persistence of its consequences on all Americans, especially those of African ancestry. They are a reminder to all who read these pages that much work still needs to be done.

TIMELINE
2001–

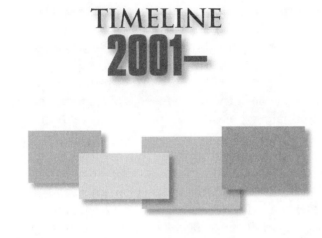

2001 In January, President-elect George W. Bush nominates Colin Powell to be Secretary of State. Condoleezza Rice takes the position of National Security Advisor for the Bush administration. This is the first time either of these posts is held by an African American.

On June 24, the Unitarian-Universalist Association, a liberal, predominantly white denomination with about 250,000 members nationwide, selects Reverend William Sinkford as its first African American president.

On July 3, Dr. Ruth J. Simmons is sworn in as president of Brown University. She is the first African American president of an Ivy League institution and the first woman president of Brown University.

On September 11, over twenty-nine hundred people die in terrorist attacks on the World Trade Center and the Pentagon. An estimated 12 percent of those killed are African Americans, Afro-Caribbeans, or Africans in what is the single deadliest attack on American soil.

The U.S. Supreme Court, in *Easley v. Cromartie,* rules that race can be considered in determining congressional redistricting plans as long as it is not the dominant and controlling decision.

In November, Shirley Clarke Franklin becomes the first African American woman to head the government of a major Southern city when she is elected mayor of Atlanta.

2002 Vonetta Flowers becomes the first African American Gold Medal winner at the Winter Olympics in Salt Lake City. She is part of a two-woman bobsled team.

In March, Halle Berry and Denzel Washington win Oscars for best actress and best actor for their portrayals in *Monster's Ball* and *Training Day,* respectively.

Serena Williams defeats her sister, Venus, in the finals of the U.S. Open, Wimbledon, and the French Open. This is the first time siblings have faced each other in these three prestigious tennis tournaments.

2003 On January 21, the U.S. Census reports that 37 million Latinos now outnumber 36.1 million African Americans. For the first time in U.S. history, blacks are no longer the largest group of color in the United States.

2004 In June, Phylicia Rashad becomes the first black woman to win a Tony Award for her portrayal of matriarch Lena Younger in the revival of Lorraine Hansberry's 1959 play, *A Raisin in the Sun.*

On November 2, Barack Obama is elected to the U.S. Senate from Illinois. He becomes the second African American elected to the Senate from that state, and only the fifth black U.S. senator in history.

2005 In January, Condoleezza Rice becomes the Secretary of State. She is the first African American woman to hold the post.

On August 30, Hurricane Katrina hits the Gulf Coast, taking an estimated seventeen hundred lives. The vast majority of the deaths are in Louisiana, including heavily African American New Orleans.

2006 Shani Davis of Chicago becomes the first black male athlete to win an individual Gold Medal in the Winter Olympics held in Turin, Italy. Davis wins his medal in the men's 1,000-meter speed skating competition.

The Covenant with Black America, edited by Tavis Smiley, climbs to No. 1 on the *New York Times* Bestseller List, making it the first black-authored book to reach No. 1 on the nonfiction paperback list.

At 7:00 a.m. on May 19, Sophia Danenberg becomes the first African American to climb to the summit of Mount Everest, the world's tallest mountain.

According to the U.S. Census Bureau, the African American population surpasses forty million on July 1.

On November 7, with the Democratic takeover of both the U.S. House of Representatives and Senate in the November midterm elections, for the first time four members of the Congressional Black Caucus chair full committees in the House: Rep. John Conyers (MI), Judiciary; Rep. Juanita Millender-McDonald (CA), House Administration Committee; Rep. Charles Rangel (NY), House Ways and Means; and Rep. Bennie G. Thompson (MS), Homeland Security.

On November 7, Deval Patrick is elected governor of Massachusetts. He becomes the second African American in the nation, after L. Douglas Wilder in Virginia in 1989, popularly elected to this position.

2007 On February 4, Super Bowl XLI pits for the first time two African American National Football League head coaches, Tony Dungy for the Indianapolis Colts and Lovie Smith for the Chicago Bears. Dungy's Colts won the game played at Dolphin Stadium in Miami, Florida, and Dungy became the first black coach to win a Super Bowl.

In May, seventy-five-year-old Harlem native and lung cancer survivor Barbara Hillary becomes one of the oldest people to reach the North Pole and is believed to be the first African American woman to accomplish that feat. Hillary, a nurse and community activist who did not know how to ski before making the journey, battled and survived lung cancer at sixty-seven.

In June, the U.S. Supreme Court, in *Parents Involved in Community Schools v. Seattle School District, No. 1,* rules that the Seattle and Louisville school administrators cannot use race as the sole factor in pupil assignments. It also declares that the promotion of racial diversity is not a compelling state interest.

On September 20, over twenty thousand march in Jena, Louisiana, to protest the arrest of six black high school students, Robert Bailey, Mychal Bell, Carwin Jones, Bryan Purvis, Jesse Ray Beard, and Theo Shaw, who were accused of beating Justin Barker, a white student at Jena High School. Related protests take place throughout the country on the same day and later there are congressional hearings. This conflict grew out of a series of racial confrontations that began in 2006 with the hanging of nooses from a tree in the high school courtyard to intimidate black students.

2008 U.S. Census Bureau projections indicate that with the surge in the Hispanic population, non-Hispanic whites will become a minority in the United States by 2042. The African American population will grow to roughly sixty million but will remain about 15 percent of the population as compared to the forty million today who comprise 14 percent.

On March 17, New York Lieutenant Governor David A. Paterson, who is legally blind, is sworn in as the governor of New York following the resignation of Governor Eliot Spitzer. Paterson is the first black governor in New York and the fourth African American in the history of the United States to serve as governor of a state.

On May 13, California Assembly representative Karen Bass is elected Speaker of the California State Assembly. Bass, who represents the Forty-seventh Assembly District (Culver City, West Lost Angeles, Westwood, Crenshaw, and Baldwin Hills), is the first African American woman chosen as speaker of any state legislature and the second black person to hold the post in California after Willie Brown.

On August 27, Illinois senator Barack Obama becomes the first African American to attain the Democratic Party nomination for President of the United States when he is chosen at the party's national convention in Denver.

On November 4, Illinois senator Barack Obama is elected the 44th President of the United States.

AFRICAN AMERICAN POPULATION OF THE UNITED STATES, 1790–2000

Year	Black Population	% of Total Population
1790	757,208	19.3
1800	1,002,037	18.9
1810	1,377,808	19.0
1820	1,771,656	18.4
1830	2,328,842	18.1

Year	Black Population	% of Total Population
1840	2,873,648	16.1
1850	3,638,808	15.7
1860	4,441,830	14.1
1870	4,880,009	12.7
1880	6,580,793	13.1
1890	7,488,676	11.9
1900	8,833,994	11.6
1910	9,827,763	10.7
1920	10,463,131	9.9
1930	11,891,143	9.7
1940	12,865,518	9.8
1950	15,044,937	10.0
1960	18,871,831	10.6
1970	22,580,289	11.1
1980	26,482,349	11.8
1990	29,986,060	12.0
2000	34,658,190	12.3

SELECTED BIBLIOGRAPHY

The following books offer additional information on the five-century history of African Americans and their background in Africa.

Altman, Susan. *Encyclopedia of African-American Heritage.* New York: Checkmark Books, 2001.

Andrews, William L., Frances Smith Foster, and Trudier Harris, eds. *The Oxford Companion to African American Literature.* New York: Oxford University Press, 1997.

Appiah, Kwame Anthony, and Henry Louis Gates, eds. *Africana: The Encyclopedia of the African and African American Experience,* 5 Volumes. New York: Oxford University Press, 2005.

Asante, Molefi K., and Mark T. Mattson. *Historical and Cultural Atlas of African Americans*. New York: Macmillan, 1992.

Bauerlein, Mark, Todd Steven Burroughs, Ella Forbes, and Jim Haskins. *Civil Rights Chronicle: The African-American Struggle for Freedom*. Lincolnwood, Ill.: Legacy, 2003.

Christian, Charles M. *Black Saga: The African American Experience: A Chronology*. Boston: Houghton Mifflin, 1995.

Ciment, James. *Atlas of African-American History*. New York: Checkmark Books, 2001.

Conniff, Michael L., and Thomas J. Davis, eds. *Africans in the Americas: A History of the Black Diaspora*. New York: St. Martin's Press, 1994.

Davis, Daren J., ed. *Beyond Slavery: The Multilayered Legacy of Africans in Latin America and the Caribbean*. Lanham, Md.: Rowman & Littlefield, 2007.

Dodson, Howard. *In Motion: The African-American Migration Experience*. Washington, D.C.: National Geographic, 2004.

Earle, T.F., and K.J.P. Lowe. *Black Africans in Renaissance Europe*. New York: Cambridge University Press, 2005.

Editors of Ebony. *Ebony Pictorial History of Black America*, 3 Volumes. Nashville, Tenn.: Southwestern, 1971.

Franklin, John Hope, and Alfred A. Moss, Jr. *From Slavery to Freedom: A History of African Americans*. New York: McGraw-Hill, 1994.

Gates, Jr., Henry Louis, and Cornel West. *The African American Century: How Black Americans Have Shaped Our Country*. New York: The Free Press, 2000.

Glazier, Stephen D., ed. *Encyclopedia of African and African-American Religions*. New York: Routledge, 2001.

Gregory, James N. *The Southern Diaspora: How the Great Migrations of Black and White Southerners Transformed America*. Chapel Hill: University of North Carolina Press, 2005.

Grun, Bernard. *The Timetables of History: A Horizontal Linkage of People and Events*. New York: Simon & Schuster, 2005.

Harris, Joseph E., ed. *Global Dimensions of the African Diaspora*. Washington, D.C.: Howard University Press, 1993.

Hawksby, Lester, Christian Humphries, and Frances Adington. *Timelines of History*. New York: Random House, 2008.

Hine, Darlene Clark, William C. Hine, and Stanley Harrold. *The African American Odyssey*. Upper Saddle River, N.J.: Pearson Prentice Hall, 2008.

Hine, Darlene Clark, and Jacqueline McLeod, eds. *Crossing Boundaries: Comparative History of Black People in the Diaspora*. Bloomington: Indiana University Press, 1999.

Hornsby, Alton, Jr., and Angela M. Hornsby. *From the Grassroots: Profiles of Contemporary African American Leaders*. Montgomery, Ala.: E-BookTime, 2006.

Ingham, John N., and Lynne B. Feldman. *African American Business Leaders: A Biographical Dictionary*. Westport, Conn.: Greenwood Press, 1994.

Irwin, Graham W. *Africans Abroad: A Documentary History of the Black Diaspora in Asia, Latin America, and the Caribbean During the Age of Slavery*. New York: Columbia University Press, 1977.

Isichei, Elizabeth Allo. *The Religious Traditions of Africa: A History.* Westport, Conn.: Praeger, 2004.

Kelley, Robin D.G., and Earl Lewis, eds. *To Make Our World Anew: A History of African Americans.* New York: Oxford University Press, 2000.

Landers, Jane, and Barry Robinson, eds. *Slaves, Subjects, and Subversives: Blacks in Colonial Latin America.* Albuquerque: University of New Mexico Press, 2006.

Levtzion, Nehemia, and Randall Lee Pouwels. *The History of Islam in Africa.* Athens: Ohio University Press, 2000.

Lipschutz, Mark R., and R. Kent Rasmussen. *Dictionary of African Historical Biography.* Berkeley: University of California Press, 1986.

Logan, Rayford W., and Michael R. Winston. *Dictionary of American Negro Biography.* New York: W.W. Norton, 1982.

Low, W. Augustus, and Virgil A. Clift, eds. *Encyclopedia of Black America.* New York: Da Capo Press, 1981.

Marmon, Shaun E., ed. *Slavery in the Islamic Middle East.* Princeton, N.J.: Markus Wiener, 1999.

McMickle, Marvin A. *An Encyclopedia of African American Christian Heritage.* Valley Forge, Pa.: Judson Press, 2002.

Miles, Tiya, and Sharon Patricia Holland, eds. *Crossing Waters, Crossing Worlds: The African Diaspora in Indian Country.* Durham, NC: Duke University Press, 2006.

Mjagkij, Nina, ed. *Organizing Black America: An Encyclopedia of African American Associations.* New York: Garland, 2001.

Painter, Nell Irvin. *Creating Black Americans: African-American History and Its Meanings, 1619 to the Present*. New York: Oxford University Press, 2006.

Plummer, Brenda Gayle. *Rising Wind: Black Americans and U.S. Foreign Affairs, 1935–1960*. Chapel Hill: University of North Carolina Press, 1996.

Ragsdale, Bruce A., and Joel D. Tresse. *Black Americans in Congress, 1870–1989*. Washington, D.C.: U.S. Government Printing Office, 1990.

Reich, Steven A. *Encyclopedia of the Great Black Migration*. Westport, Conn.: Greenwood Press, 2006.

Ripley, C. Peter, ed. *The Black Abolitionist Papers*, 5 Volumes. Chapel Hill: University of North Carolina Press, 1985–1992.

Samuels, Wilfred D. *Encyclopedia of African-American Literature*. New York: Facts on File, 2007.

Savage, Beth L., ed. *African American Historic Places: National Register of Historic Places*. New York: John Wiley & Sons, 1994.

Shillington, Kevin. *Encyclopedia of African History*, 3 Volumes. New York: Fitzroy Dearborn, 2005.

———. *History of Africa*. London: Macmillan, 1995.

Singh, Nikhil. *Black Is a Country: Race and the Unfinished Struggle for Democracy*. Cambridge, Mass.: Harvard University Press, 2004.

Smith, Jessie Carney. *Black Firsts: 4,000 Ground-breaking and Pioneering Historical Events*. Detroit, Mich.: Visible Ink Press, 2003.

Stewart, Jeffrey C. *1001 Things Everyone Should Know AboutAfrican American History.* New York: Doubleday, 1996.

Taylor, Quintard, ed. *From Timbuktu to Katrina: Readings in African-American History,* 2 Volumes. Boston: Thomson-Wadsworth, 2008.

———. *In Search of the Racial Frontier: African Americans in the American West, 1528–1990.* New York: W.W. Norton, 1998.

Teeple, John B. *Timelines of World History.* London: DK, 2006.

Trotter, Joe William, Earl Lewis, and Tera W. Hunter. *African American Urban Experience: Perspectives from the Colonial Period to the Present.* New York: Palgrave Macmillan, 2004.

UNESCO. *General History of Africa.* London: Heinemann Educational Books and University of California Press, 1981–1993.

Vogel, Joseph O., and Jean Vogel. *Encyclopedia of Precolonial Africa: Archaeology, History, Languages, Cultures, and Environments.* Walnut Creek, Calif.: AltaMira Press, 1997.

Wilson, Dreck Spurlock, ed. *African American Architects: A Biographical Dictionary, 1865–1945.* New York: Routledge, 2004.

Winks, Robin W. *The Blacks in Canada: A History.* Montreal: McGill-Queen's University Press, 1997.

Wood, Betty. *Slavery in Colonial America, 1619–1776.* Lanham, Md.: Rowman & Littlefield, 2005.

ACKNOWLEDGMENTS

America I AM Black Facts is the consequence of the efforts of a number of dedicated people. First on that list is George Tamblyn, who years ago persuaded me of the importance of timelines to students of history and who encouraged me to develop one for my faculty Web site. George scoured library and Internet sources to craft the forerunner of the project you see today. I want to thank my research assistant, Casey Nichols, who spent countless hours in research libraries and online locating documents. Casey discovered events that I might have overlooked and was particularly diligent and dedicated in the final weeks of volume preparation. In a real sense, this work owes a great deal to her efforts.

I also express my appreciation to fellow historians and social scientists Saheed Adejumobi, Seattle University; Albert

Broussard, Texas A&M University; Ronald Coleman, University of Utah; Willi Coleman, University of Vermont; George Cotkin, California Polytechnic State University, San Luis Obispo; Maceo C. Dailey, University of Texas, El Paso; Nora Lee Frankel of the American Historical Association; James Gregory, University of Washington; Donald Grinde, State University of New York at Buffalo; Richard Johnson, University of Washington; Richard S. Kirkendall, University of Washington; Dwayne Mack, Berea College; John H. McClenden, Michigan State University; James Mohr, University of Oregon; Shirley Ann Wilson Moore, California State University, Sacramento; Kevin Mulroy, University of Southern California; H. Viscount Nelson, University of California, Los Angeles; Thomas J. Pressly, University of Washington; Vincente Rafael, University of Washington; Wilson Ed Reed, Seattle University; Johnetta Richards, San Francisco State University; Greg Robinson, University of Quebec at Montreal; Herbert Ruffin, Syracuse University; Wilfred Samuels, University of Utah; Malik Simba, Fresno State University; Alonzo Smith, Montgomery College; Clarence Spigner, University of Washington; Martin Summers, University of Texas; Midori Takagi, Western Washington University; Joe William Trotter, Carnegie Mellon University; Elwood Watson, East Tennessee University; Matthew Whitaker, Arizona State University; Claytee White, University of Nevada, Las Vegas; and Gary Zellar, University of Saskatchewan.

I am grateful to the staff of various libraries and research facilities, including the Library of Congress, the University of Oregon Libraries, the University of Washington Libraries, and especially the ever-supportive staff of the UW's Interlibrary Loan Library. I am also especially appreciative of the efforts of Robert Fikes, the reference librarian at San Diego State University. I gratefully acknowledge the crucial assistance of my department head, Kent Guy, who always seemed to find resources to support this project, and to Kay

Bullitt, who always seemed to have choice words of encouragement and support at crucial times in the development of this project.

I want to thank Cheryl Woodruff for recognizing this project as a potentially useful addition to the growing body of literature on African American history, and to Tavis Smiley, whose America I AM: The African American Imprint traveling museum exhibit provided the backdrop and context for this volume. I also want to acknowledge my gratitude to the staff of SmileyBooks and copy editor Muriel Jorgensen for guiding the manuscripts through the publication process. I also acknowledge the considerable Internet research skills my daughter, Jamila Taylor, brought to this project.

Finally, I am grateful for the patience, support, and wise counsel of Catherine Dever Foster. You were a constant source of inspiration, encouragement, and love throughout this entire project.

ABOUT THE AUTHOR

Quintard Taylor, Ph.D., is the Scott and Dorothy Bullitt Professor of American History at the University of Washington, Seattle. A preeminent scholar of African American history in the American West, Taylor is the author of several books, including *In Search of the Racial Frontier: African Americans in the American West 1529–1990*.

As cofounder of the extensive online resource BlackPast.org, Taylor has helped bring African American history to every classroom in the world. Ranked #1 by Google in its category, BlackPast.org features 3,000 pages of content, seven major illustrated timelines, encyclopedia entries, and links to digital archive collections, African American museums, and research centers. Taylor lives in Seattle, Washington.

We hoped you enjoyed this SMILEYBOOKS publication.
If you would like to receive additional information,
please contact:

SMILEYBOOKS

Distributed by:

Hay House, Inc.
P.O. Box 5100
Carlsbad, CA 92018-5100

**(760) 431-7695 or (800) 654-5126
(760) 431-6948 (fax) or (800) 650-5115 (fax)
www.hayhouse.com® • www.hayfoundation.org**

Published and distributed in Australia by: Hay House Australia
Pty. Ltd. • 18/36 Ralph St. • Alexandria NSW 2015 • *Phone:*
612-9669-4299 • *Fax:* 612-9669-4144 • www.hayhouse.com.au

Published and distributed in the United Kingdom by:
Hay House UK, Ltd. • 292B Kensal Rd., London W10 5BE • *Phone:*
44-20-8962-1230 • *Fax:* 44-20-8962-1239 • www.hayhouse.co.uk

Published and distributed in the Republic of South Africa by:
Hay House SA (Pty), Ltd., P.O. Box 990, Witkoppen 2068 •
Phone/Fax: 27-11-467-8904 • orders@psdprom.co.za •
www.hayhouse.co.za

Published and Distributed in India by: Hay House Publishers
India, Muskaan Complex, Plot No. 3, B-2, Vasant Kunj,
New Delhi 110 070 • *Phone:* 91-11-4176-1620 •
Fax: 91-11-4176-1630 • www.hayhouse.co.in

Distributed in Canada by: Raincoast • 9050 Shaughnessy St.,
Vancouver, B.C. V6P 6E5 • *Phone:* (604) 323-7100 •
Fax: (604) 323-2600